AF470730
9780540009511O.

East Anglia from the Sea

"There y'are, Joe – full moon, so the old 'uns are at it again."

East Anglia from the Sea

Canvey Island to Great Yarmouth

David and Joan Hay

EDWARD STANFORD LONDON

Edward Stanford Limited
12-14 Long Acre, London WC2E 9LP
First Published 1972

ISBN 540 00951 2

Acknowledgements

In trying to give a little pleasure to our readers, I am only too well aware that we are really only making a feeble effort to repay a debt that Joan and I owe to so many people who have coloured our wandering lives.

I am thinking, not only of authors, living or long since dead, but of the companionship of old friends who have warmed our lives and left us better for having known them; of chance acquaintances in strange ports who have opened windows to new worlds of enjoyment and endeavour.

We would also like to thank Robert and Wendy Ballantine for their help over Aldeburgh illustrations and both John and his father Bill Howes of Danbury – my old schoolfriend and an Essex connoisseur – for their kindly labours at Wivenhoe on a cold winter's day.

Lastly, among the many friends who have sailed with us in *Kala Sona* over the years, and hence contributed to this series of coastal books more than they know, I shall, I hope, be forgiven for mentioning by name Anne Wallace for her delightful illustrations, and Enid and Rom Redfern who 'updated' us, as the Americans would say, on the Harwich Pubs – amongst other things.

Contents

Illustrations

Introduction

It is not easy to capture the elusive charm of the Essex and Suffolk coasts and then to reduce them to words. If you have spent even one summer among the creeks you will know for yourself, and you will agree that the vehicle of language is quite inadequate to convey the bird song of lonely saltings and the evening light when the sea lavender is in full bloom.

If you have not yet ventured round from the more sophisticated way of life along the South coast, I think you will find the experience rather worth while, and I will try and tell you why. Of course there are problems; but isn't this why we sail? If we were not looking for something a little different from our daily office life we wouldn't bother to take holidays, and if we didn't enjoy pitting our wits against the elements we would never leave our home estuaries to see what goes on round the corner and, when we feel more competent, over the horizon.

Now, before we go up the coast, or indeed any further in this appraisal of the East coast as it is in 1972, let me sketch in the other side of the picture also, in order to achieve a balanced perspective. The coast of Essex may seem a bit too near London for comfort these days, in that access is easy for its teeming millions of commuters but fortunately they tend to concentrate in Burnham and West Mersea. Where I am going to take you, I think you will agree, you might be in the Outer Hebrides except that the fishing boats have a decided East coast stamp, with still a sprinkling of Colchester smacks and bawleys. Even the brent geese haven't yet heard tell of threatened airports. Perhaps that is why it would be a good thing to enjoy the creeks while there is yet time.

There will be mud; mud in all colours of the rainbow from sandy-green to jet black and indigo blue, and it will stick to the flukes of your anchor and follow you into the waterside inn on the soles of your half-boots, but it all washes off – in time; and indeed, the changing lights of a late evening on the estuary edges are one of the unforgettable delights of a last whisky and ginger ale in the cockpit before you turn in.

If you are a gregarious type you will need an outboard on your dinghy – but so you do almost anywhere nowadays. Unless you are lucky enough to pick up a mooring where the owner is away cruising, you may have to push over a strong tide to reach the pub and with four up this is beyond the powers of most normal mortals.

There are only two marinas as yet, so you will have to rely more often on your own capabilities when the engine goes wrong or the cabin table needs repairing. But you will find every one most friendly and far more understanding because of this. It is a yachtsman's world, where you also meet landsmen – farming, fishing, bird watching or just driving to the coastal inn for an evening's fun. The South coast tends to be a holiday picnic area where yachtsmen are tolerated for their scenic value.

I must, in all fairness, mention one other local peculiarity: whereas along the coast to the south and west of our island, the rocks and underwater hazards tend to stay put, so that with a good chart you have only yourself to blame if you clot it, ours move about quite inconsequentially on occasion. Entrance bars build up in one storm and depart down-stream, unannounced, in the wake of the next. Nodules of tough shingle arrive quite uncharted in the channel and wait for you, as hard as granite, just out of sight at LWS when you are trying to beat the darkness and creep into the Deben or the Alde where the buoys and 'meets' are unlit.

This is no new problem; William Blaeu writing his *Light of Navigation* in 1608 wrote of the Southern end of this area:-

> "Goodwin is steepe and uneven, for at one casting of the lead you shall have 26 fathoms and at another cast of the lead you shall be fast upon the sand...."

Life has become a lot easier of course with electronic echo sounders, but the basic problem is still there.

Overall, it must be said that the sea is shallow a long way out and storms very quickly beat up nasty, slab-sided waves and steep seas, but against this we are well sheltered from the prevailing winds and have a lot of sunshine, if a somewhat colder climate. But no Atlantic rollers ever reach us and we have plenty of notice of gales as they work their way up the channel on the weather man's forecasts. When they do strike, there are still hundreds of miles of good sailing in sheltered waters, and no high hills or wooded cliffs to start up willy-waws and spoil a good reach.

I can't think of any more disadvantages but, on the credit side, the joys of the East coast are so many that I need only pick out a few to pass you more than a flavour of why we go back there year after year, and why, after our usual three months 'foreign' cruise, we return thankfully to anchor far from human habitation and agree that the sea birds never sing so hauntingly, even among the Danish Islands, as they do when the tide uncovers the muddy banks and seaward saltings of the Deben or Potton Creek. As the light fails we watch the old heron about his business of the evening meal, a whooper swan trumpets and when it is too dark to see any more, you can hear the wing beats of the first brent geese returning from their northern breeding places.

Inland Essex may be disappearing under motorways and housing estates, but the lonely marshes of the coastal creeks are still mystical and retain the primeval simplicity of the bygone times long before the Romans came and started all this civilization nonsense. Land and sea are of one colour in Essex and that colour changes with the light. There is a silence and a repose about the saltings, where even the rushes are a-twitter in anticipation of a breeze that will put them into a pantomime of terror as they bend and gesticulate under the dark bank beyond the moonlit water. I expect Pan started it all when he played sweet disturbing music on their forefathers.

When I think of Essex, I think of those places you can still reach by water in your own little sailing-boat and of the village inns within a short walk from the riverside hard. I am a firm believer in the old adage,

"That malt does more than Milton can
To justify God's ways to man"

The essence of the East coast is simple and local: for me it is always two villages joined by a shimmering strip of wandering waterway.

Why not try it? You will either fall under the spell of its subtle charm or you will throw this book overboard, wipe the mud off your sea boots and rapidly work out your return course across the East Swin, Middle Deep and Black Deep to the Edinburgh Channel, from where you are clear away round the North Foreland with nothing but sea between you and the sanitary pontoons and sophistication of Chichester Yacht Harbour.

One thing is certain, you cannot be indifferent about the East coast; it will become part of you or you will decide East coasters are nuts.

The Lower Thames

Anyway, in case you are prepared to try it, I will take you up the Essex and Suffolk coasts from about Canvey Island, where the Thames River proper opens out and still gives you room to sail in spite of the density of the commercial traffic coming in and out. I expect you will have with you the Stanfords Coloured Chart, the Thames Pilot and Jack Coote's *East Coast Rivers* which is a very practical aid. In passing, I had better say that we are not ignoring the Kent coast, but are going to include the Medway and Sheppey Island in a separate book.

Holehaven

Holehaven on Canvey Island has rather ceased to exist as an attractive yachting centre. In the dim past it was a sort of swamp, intersected by innumerable muddy creeks and gulleys; it has now become a bungaloid swamp, intersected by muddy drains and you may find little room in this once popular anchorage during the season. It is still, however, a possible refuge from bad weather if you can find somewhere to anchor between the oil tanks on the western corner of Canvey Island and those at Shell Haven higher up. Have a good look at your chart, because you will see that the entrance dries out, except a narrow, winding channel where you will find five foot of water at LWS abreast of the beacon. If you have to use it as a refuge, *The Lobster Smack,* beloved of Dickens, is still waiting for you hospitably on the east side of the fairway, which is the best anchorage. Afterwards you can also get water from their yard and there is good shopping in Canvey Village about a mile away.

Leigh-on-Sea

A little further down it is worth having a look in at Leigh-on-Sea, especially if you have a shallow draught, East coast boat with a centreboard, as we have. As you will find, the whole of the foreshore in front of Leigh, Westcliffe and Southend dries out soon after half-ebb, but the

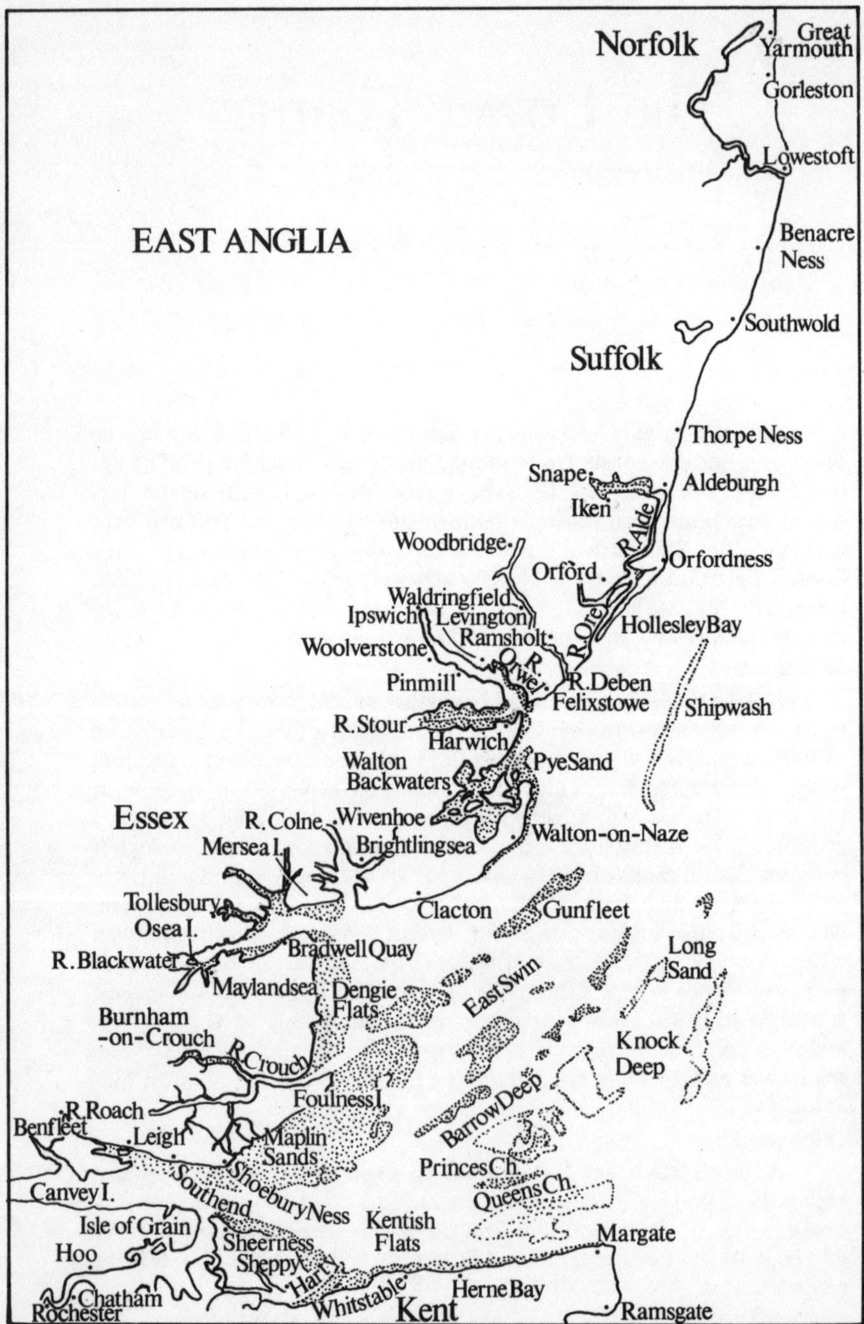
Norfolk
Great Yarmouth
Gorleston
Lowestoft
EAST ANGLIA
Benacre Ness
Southwold
Suffolk
Thorpe Ness
Snape
Aldeburgh
Iken
R.Alde
Woodbridge
Orford
Orfordness
Waldringfield
Ipswich
Levington
Ramsholt
R.Ore
HollesleyBay
Woolverstone
R. Orwel
Pinmill
R.Deben
Felixstowe
Shipwash
R.Stour
Harwich
Walton Backwaters
PyeSand
Essex
R.Colne
Wivenhoe
Brightlingsea
Walton-on-Naze
Mersea I.
Tollesbury
Clacton
Gunfleet
Osea I.
R.Blackwater
Bradwell Quay
Long Sand
Maylandsea
Dengie Flats
East Swin
Burnham -on-Crouch
R.Crouch
Knock Deep
Foulness I.
Barrow Deep
R.Roach
Benfleet
Leigh
Maplin Sands
Princes Ch.
Canvey I.
Southend
ShoeburyNess
Queens Ch.
Isle of Grain
Kentish Flats
Margate
Hoo
Sheerness
Sheppy
Harty
Chatham
Rochester
Whitstable
Herne Bay
Kent
Ramsgate

winding creek does enable you still to reach the quays at Old Leigh from the 'Low-Way' buoy about three quarters of a mile west of Southend Pier. As you go up Ray Gut, which turns into Hadleigh Ray and Leigh Creek, you may see the delightful, little cockling fleet hurrying home with their catch, probably using sweeps to work their bawleys up on the first of the flood. There are leading lights, but I don't really advise a night entrance. Once at Bell Wharf I can assure you there is no shortage of public houses, chandlers and shops, or if the Sailing Club is open they are also very welcoming.

Today, much of Southend as a seaside resort savours of the music hall, but I like to remember what a busy place it must have been in Roman times. They don't seem to have landed there, wise men, because of the mud and marshes. Indeed, in their day there was really no firm ground downstream of old London itself where a settlement could be built with any prospect of remaining above ground. But the Trinovantes tribesmen, fiddling with their slings and arrows, must have watched the great galleys anchoring far out in the stream, waiting for the tide to waft the tired oarsmen up to London, much as the Scandinavian timber boats and banana boats from the Bahamas do now.

The Elizabethan historian Camden describes Leigh as 'a pretty little town stocked with lusty seamen', and indeed the jumble of roofs still looks a bit like the backdrop for a film. The old *Ship Inn* survives, reminiscent of Gotty and other famous bare-fist fighters, but in Camden's time it was also described as 'a very proper place where tall ships do ride'. Nowadays, as well as the cocklers, you will see a certain amount of trawling for shrimps, whitebait and sprats as the seasons come round. The picturesque cutter-rigged, boomless, Leigh bawleys with their long gaffs still work the coast as far as the Maplin Sands. The cockle boats, like the mussel fishermen of Brittany, simply drive ashore and when the tide leaves them high and dry they rake the cockles into heaps, shovel them into the 'well' of their boat, until the tide puts an end to operations and they churn off home with the engine flat-out. Then the big coppers filled with boiling water are crammed full of cockles in wire bags, just as they have always been since Elizabethan times. The hot water opens the shells and in a few minutes the fish are cooked. All that is needed then is the statutory pepper pot and a vinegar bottle with a hole in the cork to season the saucerful of shrimps, prawns, and other bits of seafood which form a sort of framework for the cockles.

There are lots of myths and traditions about the place; indeed it is said the original *Mayflower* was built there, but in all due deference to Devon, there seems to be curiously, little supporting evidence. The Norsemen used both this and Benfleet as their main strongholds and in the 15th century there was founded here *'A Guild of Thames Pilots'*, later to be amalgamated with another at Deptford under the charming title *'The Fraternity of the most glorious and indivisible Trinity and St. Clement.'* From this we get our present institution of Trinity House.

Cocklers at Leigh-on-Sea

Working with cockles aboard a Leigh Cockler

Aerial view of the waterfront at Burnham on the River Crouch. *(Photo – Aerofilms)*

Up Coast to the Crouch

The Maplin Sands and Foulness

As we leave Southend Pier behind us and round Shoeburyness past the measured mile and along the Maplin Sands en route for the Crouch and its attendant tributaries to the south, one can't help thinking of the future of Foulness Island and the long past of this curiously remote and 'other worldly' bit of almost uninhabited marshland. It is a slow run up to the buoy with the delightful name of Blacktail Spit and there is time for thought. Indeed it must have been an ideal place for the original Iberian and later Celtic tribes that inhabited the area, because all the rivers and creeks behind the seaward marshes provided them with easy communication in their dug-out canoes and little wicker-work fishing boats. Then, of course, the Romans had to come and organise everybody. After which, Saxon farmers from the Friesian Islands began wandering across with their more efficient implements and opened up the heavier soil along the estuaries where they built their great wooden barnlike farm-houses. As we sail along I can't help wondering how they ever made any accurate sort of landfall, especially in dirty weather. All I can see is a slightly darker line where the low land on Foulness joins the Maplin sands which are submerged at high water. It's a featureless sort of coast all the way up to Aldeburgh, and at that time there would be no buoys or navigational aids. The Saxons hadn't, of course, heard of the compass, and in the general overcast skies prevalent in the North Sea even the stars were not always readily available as a guide. So they developed the enchanting habit of taking some poor wretched old man with them in their wind-swept, open boats, one who had already been to that part of the coast on some previous expedition. He, poor chap, soaking wet and numb with cold, was expected to explain to the oarsmen which way they should turn along the coast and how to get over the worst of the bars without being swamped. They made things slightly easier for themselves by carrying sufficient oarsmen – about 8 a side on a shift basis – to provide the manpower to carry the boat up a beach if a gale threatened, or over the shallows if it stuck on one of the shingle bars. But, my word, it must have been a fairly beastly business, with no cooking facilities and no dry cabin for the watch off-duty. If you got wet, you simply waited for the sun to come out and dry you up.

Anyway, if the weather lifts a bit you will see the radio masts at East Wick and a conspicuous Church Spire behind them as you sail on up the West Swin between the West Barrow Sands and the old lighthouse, now destroyed. After the Maplin Spit and the North East Maplin you can creep round the eastern end of Foulness sand by the familiar old Whitaker Beacon where one turns into the Whitaker Channel and beats down the five miles to the Crouch. I say 'beats' because the wind is always adverse and strong! I don't seem to remember any time when we have sailed up the Crouch with either a beam or a quartering wind. But it's always fun, especially if you avoid sitting on the Buxley Sands as we have all been known to do at one time or another. Incidentally, if you do clot it, it's quite hard and you can go for a walk as soon as the tide leaves you high and dry, but don't forget, as we nearly did once, that a sea fog or thick mist can come down very quickly, and as some three or four miles of sand dry out at low water, there would be very little chance of finding your yacht again. Added to which there is about eight foot of water over the highest point at high tide, so you would have to be very tall to keep your head above water.

The Crouch Entrance

By the time you reach the Sunken Buxey Buoy, where a coastline of sorts is emerging all round and your chart tells you that the river entrance is only two miles away, you may be starting to think about that pint in the local. But, you are not quite home yet, and in the evening, when the sun is low and straight in your eyes, it is impossible to see any sort of gap in the sands and low shores. Even if you think you know the way in, it is very easy to run slap aground on the Ray Sands – a pity when you are looking forward to a pleasant evening ashore further up the river and especially if a wind gets up before the tide refloats you during the night. So do set just one more compass course and keep to it until you can spot the Outer Crouch Buoy and the entrance.

Once into the Crouch, things get more human again and you leave the rather eerie mixture of sand and wind and sea for the sight of green meadows and flowers on river banks – not that the sea walls on the Crouch are very beautiful, but they give you a sense of shelter and homeliness, and promise of a new world round the corner. About two miles inside the river you will see the Roach running at right-angles on the port-hand side. You can anchor just inside and have complete shelter from the prevailing sou'westers or, as we are going to do now, run on into some quiet anchorage like Paglesham.

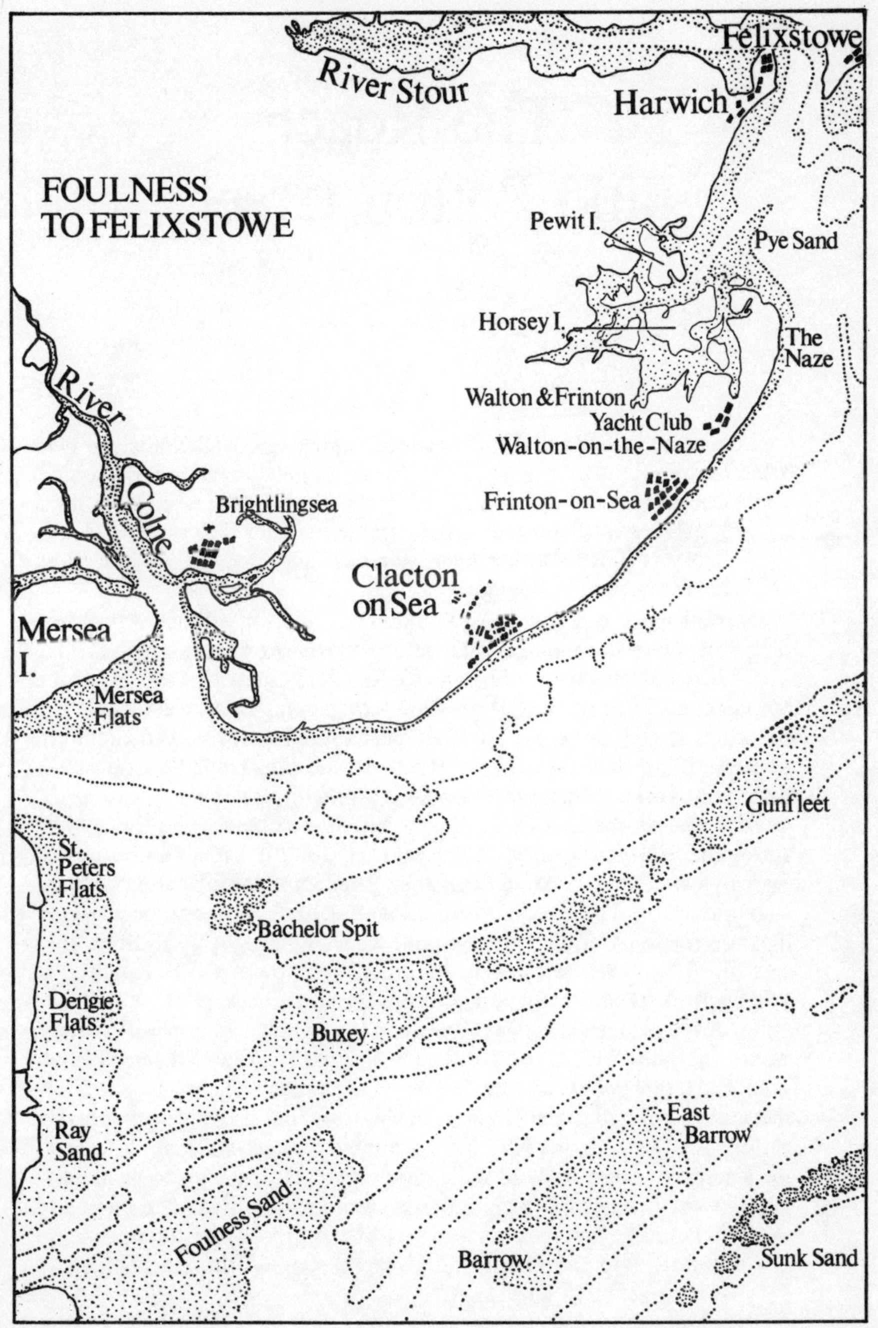
FOULNESS
TO FELIXSTOWE
River Stour
Felixstowe
Harwich
Pewit I.
Pye Sand
Horsey I.
The
Naze
Walton & Frinton
Yacht Club
Walton-on-the-Naze
Frinton-on-Sea
River
Colne
Brightlingsea
Clacton
on Sea
Mersea
I.
Mersea
Flats
Gunfleet
St.
Peters
Flats
Bachelor Spit
Dengie
Flats
Buxey
East
Barrow
Ray
Sand
Foulness Sand
Barrow
Sunk Sand

The Roach and Potton Creek

As you sail down Quay Reach on the Roach, Wallasea Island is to starboard, famous in Roman times for its oysters which the discriminating Romans spoke of as 'Wall fleets'. Later Norden was to refer to them as 'full little oysters' and that indefatigable traveller Defoe wrote,

> 'On this shoar also are taken the best and nicest, though not the largest oysters in England.'

Well, you've got to go to Pyefleet opposite Brightlingsea for them now, but the oyster men get a bit tetchy if you drop anchor in the beds.

After turning west along Devil's Reach and past Yokesfleet, which we will come back to later, Paglesham Reach turns south west where the moorings start and there is always a clear space left for you to anchor in a couple of fathoms just off the little hard that runs up to Shuttlewood's famous boat-shed. Famous, I am sure you will remember if you know anything about the East coast, for the building of barges and then, when times changed at the turn of the century, for the little, flat-bottomed 'barge-yachts' that depended on their beam for stability and could sit bolt upright on the Essex mud for a quiet night. You had to be a pygmy or a contortionist to live in them, but we were brought up to think that was fun fifty years ago, and in the immortal words of E.F. Knight, 'If you want to stand upright, you can always go on deck'.

Anyway, here is as near a yachtsman's paradise as you will get anywhere in the world. Not a habitation in sight, just an old tarred boatshed and a few yachts and fishing boats beginning to lie over on shallow moorings, while half a mile away, in the trees that provide such a lovely setting for the anchorage, is the hospitable *Plough and Sail.* You walk up a narrow country lane with the cottage gardens ablaze with gillyflowers and hedgerows thick with red campion, toadflax, storksbill and wild chamomile. Just as you turn left at the top, before the pub, there is a minute village shop which still sells everything from a teacloth to a gob stopper. It also does duty as a post office for the half dozen cottages which make up East End, as the hamlet is strictly called.

I used to come here as a boy, to this land of coppices and cornfields, where the sky and the marshes and lush meadows meet and become one entity. Though to the north there are villages on wooded slopes and hamlets at the end of the creeks, with their manor houses and old Churches, from here across to Wakering saltings there are only the scattered cottages of the marsh dwellers nursing old customs and superstitions; and the pleasant thing is that it is there still, in spite of threats of new aerodromes and London only 35 miles away. No highroads in this empty land stretch long and straight to the nearest town.

The Plough & Sail at Paglesham

As I sit in the *Plough and Sail* at East Paglesham fifty years seem to drop away as naturally as an oakleaf falls in the autumn. Even the dialect that I remember is still there: the dialect of the Essex fisherman and men of the marshland farms. It is an old language and still retains much of the original Saxon. If you listen, you can pick up words used by Chaucer and Langland mixed with Friesian Dutch or plat Deutsch and bits of Norman that settled into our language, but have since been lost to the rest of England. It is a harsh language with the 'a' pronounced the way it is in Australia today, and often the 'w' and 'v' transposed and the strong form, instead of the weak form in the past tenses, such as 'gove' for given, rep for reaped and snew for snowed. Here you can still hear 'housen' used instead of houses, 'fleet' is still used for 'shallow' and 'hazardable' for 'dangerous'. But above all, I like 'dewbit' for the ploughman's early breakfast and 'beaver' for his lunch, 'onsensed' for 'stunned', 'dooles' for wayside heaps of hay, and 'onbeknown' is not used in jest.

When you are tired of drinking and listening – or eating, if you have a mind to, for there are delicious snacks or freshly cut sandwiches – back to the yacht before it gets dark because, if you are like us, there is always a bit of snugging down to be done on deck before the light goes and you can get down to a pipe and a book or a bridge four in a cosy cabin.

Even that half mile back to the anchorage has an enchantment all of its own, for it is in the late evening that the hedgerow smells are at their sweetest. And Essex is a county of hedgerows as well as saltings; I think they last in my memory as well as any of the more obvious or spectacular features. Here the ditches are choked with sweet-smelling plants that fill the night air with their fragrance as you tread on them; with lords and ladies, hemlock, Queen Anne's lace, rest harrow, shepherd's purse, sea sand spurrey and wild mignonette. Wild campion is there and loosestrife and the crumbly meadowsweet that I remember most from boyhood rambles, the flower beloved of the long green and red beetles whose name escapes me – if I ever knew it.

Generations of birds have been hatched in this half mile of hedgerow and in the nettles at its feet. The white-throat slings its flimsy apology of a dried-grass nest between the middle stems, and now and then you will find the really well-tailored residence of the reed-warbler if you are lucky. The whitethroat, especially in June, hardly ever seems to leave his nest; he hops up to the top of the hedge, sings his silvery, swelling little song and goes back home to watch us go by. Bullfinches will sit in the thickest part of the thorn bushes and placidly watch the activity along the dusty lane. It is a pity most yachtsmen lay up by the end of September, for the late October hedges are a riot of colour; pride of place being taken by the hedge maple, whose range of brilliant yellow tints would be hard to imitate in watercolours.

Back aboard, the estuary is very quiet, as it always is about sun down. The day birds are going to bed and the night birds haven't begun or are too busy feeding if the tide is out. This time is pleasant sitting in the cockpit; I like it because you can distinguish the sounds when there are not so many. There is a cow sounding lost in a distant meadow, then the 'cruik' of a moorhen closer by. Farm noises carry a great distance when it is still, especially over water. You can hear a dog bark or even a farmyard hen at about two miles. You can often hear the unmistakable 'tweet' of hunting tits in the bushes on the bank and the soft 'clap' of a homing pigeon landing in the woods – quite different from the smart clap of wings over his back in flight, which is such a feature of the spring courtship flight. Not many birds glide; a heron you will probably see, moving from one favourite fishing corner to the next, almost like an albatross with his huge, cupped vanes of wings. But the old starling is not a bad performer and as a boy I watched him with great envy. It all seemed such an effortless way to wander around the world. All sea birds glide well – they have to – but of the land birds you meet up the Essex estuaries only those with short rounded wings do so easily, birds such as owls, partridges, pheasants and hawks. Long after it is too dark to see, you can have a lot of fun analysing the typical night noises. Apart from curlews and oyster-catchers there is little bird song, but sometimes, in season, you may catch the nightingale (though he tends to favour Suffolk these days!) and the sedge-warbler. To interpret the rustles and clicks and faint subdued rustlings that make up the evening silences, you have to be a fairly good naturalist and know the habits of the little hunting animals in search of dinner, but that is why it is such fun to learn, for there is always something new and by the time you get a bit long in the tooth for tough foreign cruising. you will have a wonderful hobby to fill your days with just as much fun as you used to have exploring new lands.

Now before we leave this no-man's land of creeks and grassy islands, you might do worse than take a turn round Potton Island. Potton Creek joins the Paglesham Reach we have been discussing, at Barling Ness. From there it wanders south for a mile or so at about a fathom LWS until, under the opening bridge you find yourself in a pleasant pool which dries out at low water by Sutton and Smith's boatyard. They are friendly folk and if you tie up and wander in you will see traditional, East coast, wooden boats still being built in clinker or carvel. Our own six and a half ton centreboarder was built there and a jolly good sea boat she is. Great Wakering is about a mile away, with four pubs to choose from and at high water you can motor up Barlinghall Creek in your dinghy, past the old, ruined barge quays almost to Barling and Little Wakering, but set out on the return journey well before half-tide,

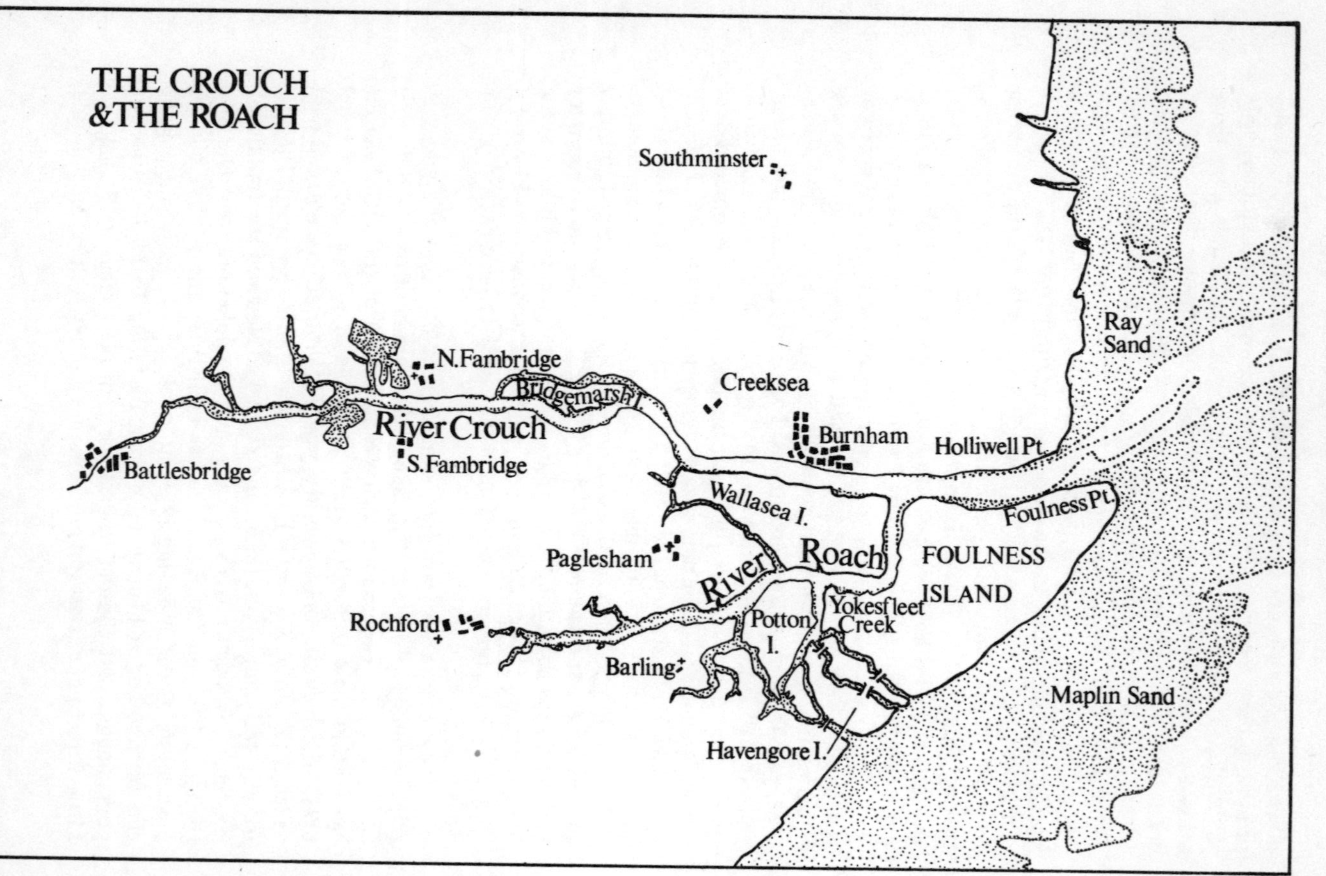
THE CROUCH
&THE ROACH
Southminster
Ray
Sand
N.Fambridge
Creeksea
Bridgemarsh I.
River Crouch
Burnham
Holliwell Pt.
Battlesbridge
S.Fambridge
Wallasea I.
Foulness Pt.
Paglesham
River Roach
FOULNESS
ISLAND
Yokesfleet
Creek
Rochford
Potton
I.
Barling
Maplin Sand
Havengore I.

as there is now no water at all at low. If you draw 3'6" or less, you can arrange for the Havengore bridge to let you through and across the Maplin sands, but I don't advise it even at Springs. The most fun is to complete the circumnavigation of Potton Island and anchor in Yokesfleet Creek just before the entrance to the Roach. This is the most sheltered anchorage I know anywhere and whatever the strength or direction of the wind you will have a quiet night.

The Crouch

Burnham

This, I suppose, is normally regarded as the most sophisticated yachting centre on the East coast; and indeed at first sight its mile or so of moorings – five or six lines of them for the river is broad here – look a bit terrifying, particularly if you arrive at a weekend when racing is in full swing. Among this clutter of moorings, anchoring is obviously out, as the fairway is narrow. But sophistication is a relative matter, and, though there are large yacht clubs, good boatyards and a Marina on the south bank, most of us still prefer to get a spare mooring from a friendly boatman and hope that a yard boat will be around if wind and tide are adverse when we are ready to go ashore.

Burnham itself is a pleasant, sleepy, old coastal town where you can buy all that you need. The landlord of the *Old White Hart* will have a noggin ready for you, together with a fund of local news and gossip if he is on form! Up the hill towards the station, the *Oyster Smack* reminds you of this all pervading occupation. I like going into Cranfield's great, wooden-floored cutting-room where our own sails were stitched, and watching the age old craft flourishing as racing, cruising or fishermen's steadying sails are still measured out and put together with the right curve for a perfect aerofoil.

The cruise up-river is pleasantly varied; there is Creeksea and a stretch of sand and wooded ridges to the north. Even if your memory of history is getting a bit shadowy, Canute should ring a bell. Like Queen Elizabeth and the number of beds she is supposed to have graced in her more sportive moments, this is one of the beaches where he found, like many of us, that the North Sea tides wait for no man. Indeed, a little further up you can see the quaint Churches of Canewdon and Ashingdon. It was on the slopes of this hill that Edmund and his Saxons hacked away for the best part of 24 hours at Canute until Edric, one of his less enthusiastic Midland allies, remembered he had a prior engagement and slipped off home. This left Canute free to complete a famous victory; a victory incidentally, which gave us all those unmemorable and unpronounceable Danish kings who having "landed correctly in Thanet" upset good King Alfred and caused him to burn Mrs. Girth's cakes in an absent-minded moment.

Fambridge

Indeed, as we are in a memorable mood you can drop anchor, yes really this time, as the moorings do not yet occupy the whole river, at Fambridge and on your way to the cosy old *Ferry Boat* inn on the north side, recall the Essex version of Lord Ullin's daughter. Here-a-ways she was called Lady Francis Rich from the Old Manor House at Rochford and she ran away with Master John Cammock, a squire of low degree – all as it should be. They got surprised when out on a so-called hawking expedition and were chased as far as Fambridge by Father, who was very wealthy and was, as usual, in the throes of moving house from the Leighs. Anyway they both jumped on John's poor horse and swam it across – some horse – and got happily wed, to everybody's satisfaction, in Maldon the same night. It seems to have done them a power of good, for they brought off thirteen children whose wooden effigies you can still see in All Saints Church, Maldon when you go up the next estuary, the Blackwater. In fact you will find all twenty-two children, if you can count that far, as our friend wasn't done yet and had another 9 by a second wife Ursula; they are all tastefully grouped together with a wife on either side of the busy little man.

Everyone is very friendly at Fambridge boatyard and if you want a convivial session, look in to the *Ferry Boat* on a Saturday evening when the locals challenge the yachting fraternity at darts, and Common Market problems become the stuff of fairy tales and nobody gives an East Anglian damn what M. Pompidou or any other of them foreigners is up to. Come to that you can go down to Fambridge any weekend in winter, and frost, rain or sun, the stoves will be going in many a laid-up yacht and the wood fire in the *Ferry Boat* will seem doubly good. There's a perfectly pleasant pub on the south side but, somehow most folk seem to prefer the north.

If a west or east wind gets up, you can drop round the corner upstream of Brandy Hole for a quiet night in complete shelter. Many years ago, we had a boat built there and I had much pleasure in recording its port of origin on the registration forms.

Well, that is just about all of the Crouch unless you run up to one of the most delightful, little, white-boarded inns in Essex, *The Barge* at

Battlesbridge, but you will have to do it by dinghy or at HWS, when you will find six or seven feet, and either have to drink rather rapidly or dry out against the mill quay for the night, and there are worse places than that. The Vikings used to do it in their long boats when they got tired of wading ashore up the slippery mud banks to try a little rape and massacre.

To the Blackwater Estuary

Now for the next area of creeks and anchorages, and it's a bit of a giggle to think that Maldon is only six miles, or an hour and a half's walk across the peninsular. By water it is about twenty-five to thirty-five miles according to the route you choose.

By this time you will, if you don't already know the East coast, have looked at the chart often enough to realise that even a short sea passage may not be the simple affair that it is along much of the South coast where, once you are clear of the immediate problems, you have nothing to worry about until you reach the other side. Here in the Thames Estuary, however, you may be fifteen to twenty miles out and still see the seagulls *walking* on parts of the Kentish Knock or the Long Sand. Coming up to the Crouch we were lucky enough to find a convenient channel close inshore, (we shall find another between the Blackwater and Harwich) but from the Crouch to the Blackwater the way is barred by two of our biggest and best sandbanks – the Buxey and the Gunfleet. If we were going straight up to Harwich it might pay to go right round the outside of the Gunfleet, but for the Blackwater this would add another twenty-five miles to our day's sail.

Fortunately a kindly Providence has taken pity on 'we poor sailormen' and arranged two small gaps in these banks – the Rays'n, between the shore and the Buxey, and the Swin Spitway, between the Buxey and the Gunfleet. Neither channel is possible at low water and both indulge in that good old East coast habit of shifting about and changing their depths every time there is a gale. So, you may feel that it is a little safer, unless you have local knowledge, to use the main channel, the Swin Spitway. It is only a mile across and marked on each side by an unmistakable, bulbous-shaped, striped buoy. If you are early on the tide you can find that the southern end is a little like Piccadilly Circus, with fishermen trying their luck off the banks, and the larger yachts and even a small coaster anchored, just as the sailing barges used to, while waiting for water. It is an eerie sensation anchoring here, apparently in the middle of the ocean, for the coast on the clearest day is no more than the faintest smudge. A deep draught boat might have to wait until near high water, but most of us will probably slip across safely at about half-tide when the current is at its strongest. Generally speaking on the East coast the tides play fair; they make down and ebb up the coast, follow the line of the coast or the main channels between the sandbanks and rarely exceed two and a half knots even at HWS. At the Spitway, however, they sluice *across* the Channel and you will find you have to crab across to avoid being swept over the banks.

The Rays'n, if you have a mind to try it, will save you ten miles and about three hours – that is assuming you weave your way without incident between the Dengie Flats on one side and the Buxey Sands on the other. There is an equally good chance that you may add hours to your day if, as we did one filthy foggy April morning when the 'conspic' Radio Masts on Foulness were invisible, you clot it and take the right course from the wrong buoy. At about 0430 hours we found ourselves well aground on Buxey; the mist cleared later and up came the Buxey Beacon two miles away, as cheerful as they make 'em. It was a long day. We got into the dinghy and played chess, I remember, with a wary eye on the weather in case it blew up.

Since those days the southern end of the Rays'n is a bit easier to find as the Burnham clubs are kind enough to put a buoy there during the season, but from there on you are on your own, with the nasty little Bachelor's Spit unmarked at the northern end and an uncertain depth of water. If you are aiming for the Rays'n it is always worth trying to get some up to date local knowledge of the likely depths as it changes so quickly. One year there can be fears that it is silting up, the next you may find, as we did in 1971, some eight or nine feet at HWN.

Once past Bachelor's Spit you can easily pick up the Bench Head or Bar Buoy and explore the Colne on the way into the Blackwater proper. The shallows can be tricky, so I should have a good look at your Stanford charts, the Cruising Association Handbook or Jack Coote's *East Coast Rivers.* Because, in addition, it can be very difficult on a day of bad visibility to distinguish anything when looking up the Blackwater River, except perhaps the Bradwell power station. A course of 295° will take you to the Nass Beacon, God willing, and on a northerly course from the Colne Bar buoy with its triangular top mast, you should soon see the group of three buoys opposite Colne Point. Generally the white conical Fishing Buoy comes up first, especially if the sun in shining.

The Colchester River

Although the Colne is, strictly speaking, outside the Blackwater River and across on the north side, I suggest we have a look at it first because it, well, it has everything – oysters, good pubs, priories, enchanting water fronts like Wivenhoe, where you might be in Holland, and old King Cole's town, Colchester, simply stuffed with historical buildings and tales of loot and seasonal rapine – all on one river, together with one of the wildest and loneliest set of marshes where the redshanks, dunlin and curlews entertain you on a quiet evening in the cockpit. What Gaumont British film blurb or packaged tour can offer all that, for free.

This is indeed the 'land of Mehalah' which Baring-Gould painted so hauntingly in his Essex classic. We think of the unhappy little soul punting her way back to the farm of her ague-riddled old Mum on Ray Island at the end of Pyefleet, with its twisted thorn-bushes bent double by the east wind and a fire of wreck-wood burning fitfully on the brick hearth.

But in the summer, when you will be sailing up the Colne, the marshes will be aglow with the shot satin of the thrift, turning to purple as the sea lavender comes into flower and every creek and pool is fringed with the sea aster. The glasswort that came up so green in the spring will by now, also have turned to every shade of carmine. Always there are the shelduck and crows and in season the brent geese – black geese as they are called in Essex. As the meadows appear over the sea wall, you can see the little white beehives among the orchards, for Essex folk are compulsive Beekeepers. On the water you will still see Thames Barges with their brown sails as most of the remaining ones, now in private hands, lie up at Maldon or Pin Mill on the Orwell and sail from one to the other fairly regularly. They are a grand sight, being the largest remaining sailing craft afloat in British waters, bar a few replicas and specially built craft like the *Winston Churchill*.

Brightlingsea

Brightlingsea is the first port of call. The channel buoys are plentiful and you will have time to watch the town come up, first the Church, then the larger sheds over St. Osyth's Point. On the port-side are the sheep farms and the saltings of Mersea Island, of which Defoe once said,

> 'Vast flights of duck, teal and widgeon abound.....indeed the creeks seem covered with them. Men of pleasure', he adds, 'journey from London to enjoy the sport and often return well laden, and with Essex ague on their backs.'

Curlews, with a whimbrel in flight

There are fewer of these birds now, but the dabchicks are still there and the coot calls across rivulets which are the haunt of the water rail – that secretive bird which is elsewhere becoming very rare. I like watching the geese as the mist lifts on still mornings and the mallard stretch their necks in the first sun. Like many of my friends, I long ago lost the urge to shoot these beautiful creatures. I can only hope the modern youth will grow up even more quickly.

Fishing smacks still anchor off Mersea Point where the shingle is hard and landing easy, and the *Dog and Pheasant* is only a mile away. But you will generally find most of the smacks anchored fore and aft by Stone Point opposite the Town Hard, where there is about five feet of water at low tide. Beyond them, withies mark the oyster beds and anchoring will land you in trouble! The harbour master will usually find you a vacant mooring and the town makes a pleasant evening's potter. If you have time, a visit by dinghy to St. Osyth Creek to see the old 12th century Priory and the remains of the old tide mill by the quay is rather fun. Or, if you prefer a quieter anchorage you can motor round to Pyefleet on the port side of the main channel, marked by a red can buoy (No.12) which, incidentally, you should leave to starboard as it is really a main channel buoy and marks a spit. There is plenty of room even these days, as far as Pewit Island in deep water and almost six feet as far as Maydays Marsh where the channel forks. This is much quieter than Brightlingsea in a strong sou'wester.

The Priory, or Abbey, really is worth a visit. The gate house, across the lawn and flowerbeds, is beautifully panelled in flint and stone, and there are fishponds and pleasant topiary. It is complete with its own ghost, the founder St. Osyth who carries her own head under her arm in the best romantic tradition. She was a fascinating character, very feminine. The daughter of the old king of Mercia, she was brought up in a convent and took the usual vow of virginity. She fell into a river with a school book in her hand and was drowned. But already she must have been marked out for a saintly future because later in the day the searchers, directed by a passing angel, called her name and she obligingly broke surface with the book intact. Like other 'with it' young ladies of the seventh century, she practised her virginity conscientiously until her parents thought it would be good for her if she married one, Sighere, the King of the East Saxons. This only lasted until the first evening, when the King started looking out of the window – always a bad sign – and seeing a splendid stag, gave chase. Mistress Osyth took umbrage, not unnaturally and remembering the virginity business, also whizzed off – to her nunnery for good. The understanding King was very decent about it and gave her the manor of Chich as a parting present, plus money to run it and to found a personal nunnery of her own.

All went swimmingly until a rather primitive Danish skipper called Hubba plundered the establishment and because they found the Prioress a thought obstinate they took her to a spot now called Nun's Wood and chopped her head off. Where the head fell, a clear spring of fresh water issued from the ground. This miracle was followed by another as the redoubtable Prioress carried her own head back to the Nunnery and knocked on the door before she fell dead. Ever since that

The 'Ferry Boat Inn' at North Fambridge on the River Crouch.

Barling Creek at the head of the River Roach.

Wivenhoe on the Colne River, Essex. A view across the River with the quay and the Church of St. Mary the Virgin beyond.

day she comes one night in each year to visit the scene of her murder – holding her head in her hands. This mixture of fact and half-forgotten legend is not only the stuff of dreams it is the background of this dream world where the sky and the Essex saltings meet, even in this twentieth century.

Wivenhoe

Back aboard, you are again in a land of yachts, sprats and oysters from which next day, you can move on the tide up-stream to the enchanting waterfront of Wivenhoe – into the heart of Essex without even having to take a walk. You can tie up to the quay right in front of a colourful waterfront with its famous boatyards and stay upright, even without legs, in the very soft mud and enjoy Colchester Natives – Pyefleets really – and see if you agree that they are 'the most succulent oysters in the world'. The Essex climate seems to suit the infant 'spat' and the locals have the art of 'laying the culch' wrapped up to a 'T'.

Just across the water in Fingringhoe Church you can see St. Michael estimating the weight of souls while perched on the spandrels of the outer doorway – quite a feat – while the Dragon presumably, is ruminating on the good old days when the Church lent an aura of sanctity to the smugglers who lodged their wares cosily in the crypt.

Colchester

Three miles above is the oldest city of the land. Colchester is a city of ghosts. The ghosts of Celtic farmers, to be followed all too surely by ghosts of the slaughtered Roman citizens when Boadicea swept through to London in the greatest massacre the southern invaders ever suffered. You can still see the black line of fire where the city was burnt to the ground. Norman followed Saxon in angry succession until it was Roman Catholic and Protestant at each other's throats. Even the smooth lawns of the public gardens, now bright with flowers, have their gallant ghosts. The old castle still frowns upon the spot where the sturdy defenders of a lost cause, Sir Charles Lucas and Sir George Lisle, cheerfully 'counted it gain to die' for a wayward king. 'Come nearer,' said Sir George to the musketeers, 'I have been much nearer, friends, when you have missed me'. They will still be the most treasured ghosts when all the Quakers and the smugglers done to death in the castle dungeons of later years are forgotten. Perhaps as well, for the town is now a cheerful place in spite of its past. Children play round the old siege house in East Street and the fallen magnificence of the Roman villas provide an appropriate enough background for twentieth century courting couples when their elders are safely stowed for the evening in the *Red Lion*.

As you return downriver from Wivenhoe the wrecks of little coasting barges and fishing boats are gradually uncovered by the falling tide. They provide no hazard if you follow the channel, but I can never

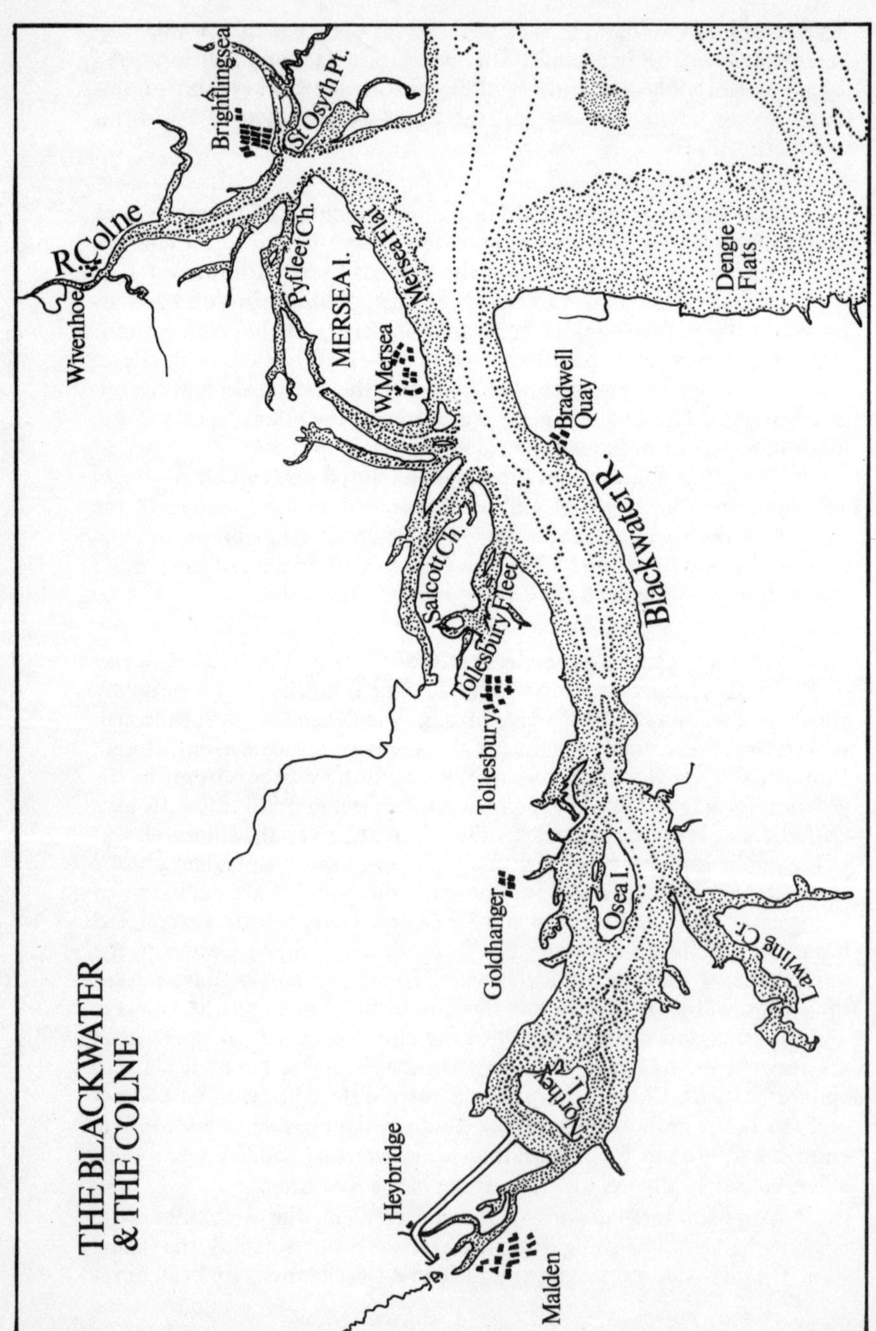
THE BLACKWATER
& THE COLNE
Brightlingsea
St Osyth Pt.
R. Colne
Wivenhoe
Pyfleet Ch.
MERSEA I.
Mersea Flat
W. Mersea
Dengie
Flats
Bradwell
Quay
Blackwater R.
Salcott Ch.
Tollesbury Fleet
Tollesbury
Goldhanger
Osea I.
Lawling Cr.
Northey
I.
Heybridge
Malden

pass these sad little relics on any shore without wondering how they came by their end and whose loving hands cared for them in the days of their working life when they breasted the North Sea gales and brought their owners safely back to shelter, times uncounted. It is odd in a way how personal the relationship becomes between man and boat until the familiar hull and spars and cabin become part of his own personality and inseparable from his being as a human entity. I don't know about the bedouin and his camel, they are ugly ill-tempered brutes at the best of times, but I certainly can't conceive the same affinity between the commercial traveller and his faithful Ford thoughtfully provided by a munificent management.

One can have a sharp reminder of this difference. Two years ago we struck an uncharted jagged reef or underwater obstruction in the mouth of an estuary on the Atlantic coast of Brittany – and sank in two minutes flat. We were lucky to be able to reach a shallow in that time and were later salvaged by the local lifeboat in the nick of time before the tide rose and swept her into deep water where she would have been lost for good. Even so, all our perishable gear and stocks for a three month's voyage were destroyed. At the time you have to put a good face on things but I will now readily admit that the sense of near loss of an old friend wasn't shaken off until long afterwards.

The Blackwater River

Anyway, enough of whimsy, here we are back at the entrance to the Blackwater River proper (the 'Pant' as it used to be called) and Maldon is ahead with its Church on the hill above the cluster of tall-masted barges gathered below on the waterfront. I have a feeling that you will enjoy this river also, once you have hoisted in the fact that in many places in its seventeen miles there is more mud than water. It has low banks so the wind is kindly and plays you no tricks; there are many safe and quiet anchorages and above all there is a feeling of spaciousness and freedom from restriction that is all its own. There is also an indefinable charm that I find hard to pin down. Perhaps it is because, to me, even a grassy promontory or islet which I can take in at a glance is exciting if you sit in the dinghy and watch it quietly for a while. The dunlins and a redshank or black-tailed godwit will come along, too busy searching the muddy waterline for food to notice you if you are still. Wild thyme grows almost down to the water's edge and the meadowbrowns and sometimes a red admiral, flutter irresolutely over the sow-thistle and yellow hawksbeard. Most of their fellows prefer the cottage gardens where the wild forget-me-nots and the pimpernels and cornflowers grow in profusion. There is shepherd's purse and, on patches of shingle, you may find the rambling sea-pea that grows so profusely further north at Shingle Street itself. I don't know if you have watched the water voles in the sort of narrow gutway that runs up into the grasses. I can't really believe all their journeyings are necessary; much of their movements, especially when in company, seem to be just for the fun of it. They have a comic way of popping out of their holes, just head and shoulders, giving you a knowing stare and popping back again to gossip. And all the time the larks and the meadow pipits are very busy above in the blue sky; the larks never taking more than about 3 minutes over their song before plummeting earthwards again.

Mersea Island

As we are already on the north shore we had better finish with Mersea Island and the Tollesbury and Goldhanger Creeks, leaving Lawling and Bradwell for the return journey. Now, although the West Mersea yacht club is hospitable and their boatman generally helpful if he can be found, it is such a popular place because of nearness to London that only a miracle will achieve a mooring and you are far more likely to find yourself anchored in the Quarters (see chart), and at the seaward end at that. This is rough in almost any sort of a wind. If you try your luck higher up I advise you to motor, whatever the good books say, as there is not room to swing a mouse between the moorings. Once in and anchored somewhere, there are all facilities and buses running inland.

The Island itself is still quite fun, that is all but the recent sprawl of villas. There are coppices alight with bluebells, primroses and celandine in the spring and the song thrush still nests in the hazel bushes. If you have a mind to potter back in time, the place still reeks of the Romans to whom it was a very convenient and easily fortified stronghold, complete with oyster beds and a good harbour. Indeed it is still a semi-amphibian country, especially to the north and west where creek succeeds creek across Pennyhole Fleet as it lies sparkling in the setting sun. But I advise exploration by dinghy unless you are fond of sitting in the mud, as once you have squeezed in you may find you can't even turn your little yacht round, and if you get jammed across a gutway on a falling tide you will not only feel a right charlie but may break her back. There are two hards in Besom Creek (Buzz'm to the local fishermen who mostly use it) and a concrete causeway off the 'Old City'.

If you hear the clash of sword on harness over Barrow hill at full moon don't be alarmed or interrupt your evening pint, it is only a couple of enthusiastic Danish brothers who fought all day over a local popsie until they dropped dead. The popsie conveniently died of sorrow and they are all three cosily buried there. Each full moon they have a sort of *resorgimento* and continue the fight with encouraging shouts until the light goes. The locals are quite used to it and merely remark, 'The old 'uns are at it again.' The island provided 'a barge and six men' to help Edward III appropriate Calais and, as you would expect the Royalists and Roundheads fought over it during the troubles. Now you will only hear the shotguns of wild fowlers and the popping of corks up and down the autumn creeks when the season opens.

But you will be tucked up in the hospitable bar of the *Victory Inn*, an old smuggler's haunt. Looking across the Virley Channel from there, or better still from the top of the old Saxon Church tower, you get a good view of the creeks and indeed if you like ditch crawling there is no better place to do it. Mind the old withy stumps as you row up Salcott

Creek to the little hamlet so named for the old trade of salt panning in the marshes when that commodity was vital for winter survival in the cottages. Opposite, is the ruin of Virley Church, 'a small, hunch-backed edifice in the last stages of delapidation' says Baring Gould a vicar of East Mersea in his *Mehalah* which I have just re-read with great pleasure. He doesn't seem to have been on the same wavelength as his parishioners but he knew his saltings and creeks and is worth reading just to hear the salt wind sing through swatchways.

Tollesbury

At Tollesbury we find another touch of South coast sophistication. Tollesbury Fleet has silted up in the last fifty years, but you can still lie afloat just short of Woodrolfe Creek, or use the new yacht harbour which now has most facilities. On the way up you will see a number of local fishing craft usually parked in what they call rather appropriately 'The Leavings'. You can get right up to Tollesbury by dinghy or land at the *Gridiron* or better still at Drake's yard where the foreshore is steep-to and walkable on. It is a quaint old village with a pleasant pub.

Goldhanger Creek

Indeed there are a number of very worthwhile little inns for a lunchtime stroll up these creeks. You could do a lot worse than try the *Thatcher's Arms* two miles away at Tolleshunt d'Arcy or the *Chequers* at Goldhanger where we will look in next day. Goldhanger is back along South Channel and round the Nass Beacon, sou'west past Thirslet Creek, four miles on. I say 'past', because I must warn you the name spoken quickly might mislead poor sailormen. There is nowhere to quench anything. It is, as far as I remember, just a creek to nowhere. But, two miles on, a black buoy announces Goldhanger Creek. It is really a main channel buoy I should warn you, and must be left to port when entering. I should run your echo sounder the first time up because although there are six feet of water for some considerable way, the hard by the village dries out and it is another dinghy job. It is an odd sensation as the water is almost as clear as the Baltic or Danish Islands. I suppose it is because of the thick weed all along the bottom. You will, maybe, have to clean your outboard prop, but even this is fun because you can watch the green crabs scuttle about the bottom while you float along, cutting off their sunlight by your shadow. The village has been described as 'a nice little village with a pump', but I like it and I hope you will enjoy your pint at the *Chequers.* They are a friendly crowd and, as often as not, share their pints while you wait for yours.

Osea Island

If it is high tide, you can motor your dinghy back round the other side of Osea Island but I don't see any point in doing so. I would much rather lie anchored by the pier on the island if the wind is right, as it is one of the most pleasant spots on a quiet evening if you are dining aboard. There will be a certain amount of coming and going along the river, especially sailing dinghies, but they only serve to accentuate the overall quiet. Ringed plovers still come here in the breeding season, and the lapwing, but most other birds have gone to less disturbed quarters.

Heybridge Basin

If you want food or provisions you can go round the corner and lock in to Heybridge Basin. It is sometimes difficult to spot whether the gates are open or closed, but once you get in line with them the lock keeper will see you coming and tell you whether he can take you at once or advise you to anchor awhile; the holding is good. The charge, according to Mr. Coote, is still less than 30p a week with a small charge for entrance.

It is possible to land on sand, at certain states of the tide at Mill Beach just before Heybridge and there is an inn but I have never landed to sample it. There is always the *Jolly Sailor* or the *Ship* further along the sea wall.

Maldon

If you want a pleasant walk after dinner, go along the 'Navigation' which gives the impression more of a Dutch canal than Essex until, about Beeleigh Abbey, the Chelmer and Blackwater meet. The flowers are nowhere lovelier; 'apple' or 'cherry-pie' willow-herb and meadow-rue, purple loosestrife, wild forget-me-not and sweet smelling hemp, line the river banks. Here and there you come across agrimony and the skull-cap, but it is the great water dock with its palm-like leaves, that sticks in one's memory even more vividly than the yellow clusters of the wild flags that are everywhere. I mention this because the rest of the way to Maldon is very, very dull. The ancient town itself, just round one bend and a wiggle from Heybridge, really needs two tides – one to arrive on and dry out against a barge or the Quay if you can find a hole, and one to leave on. Otherwise you will see no more of the town than you have done already from Osea, when the sun went down behind Maldon hill, and the Church and old houses stood out black against the evening sky.

On the way up the hill from the Hythe you pass St. Mary's Church. The old beacon on the tower that was lit for ships coming up the estuary has long since gone, in fact the whole tower fell down in Charles I's time and the replacement is not very beautiful. If you fall to talking in one of the pleasant inns you will hear the Song of Maldon telling you the defeat of Brithnoth by the Danes who then occupied the town and established their main stronghold at Danbury a few miles to the west on the highest hill in Essex. I cannot do better than quote Miss Julia Cartwright writing in the *Essex Review* many years ago as if from the windy slopes of Lingwood,

'Here, on these heathery slopes, when the wild rose and honeysuckle hang in clusters from the briars, and the ground is carpeted with sweet smelling thyme and starry yellow saxifrage, we have one of the loveliest views of Danbury. We see the tall spire of its ancient Church rising above the red roofs of the old houses that creep up the hillside and we look across the heather and bracken to the woods of Riffhams Chase – the manor owned by Earl Godwin in Saxon times – and the wide plains that stretch far away to Colchester and London'.

The waterfront at Maldon

She has it in a nutshell – and the pleasant thing is that it might have been written today. You can take a bus up for the day and I think you will agree it is an enchanted spot, once away from the main road with its new shoddy houses.

Anyway back in Maldon, do go and have a drink in the *Blue Boar* and don't be put off by appearances. Once inside you see the old coaching yard, still surrounded by timbered buildings as fine as any you are likely to see on your cruise. Incidentally, most of its earlier customers seem to have found a final niche opposite in All Saints Church – what a grand and almost unique, triangular tower! Brithnoth is of course there, looking as fit as a flea for all his years. Bishop Cedde and the whole string, all twenty-two, of the Cammock progeny I referred to when at Fambridge. There is even the great, great grandfather of George Washington, complete with a window presented by citizens of modern America.

I could fill many pages with stories of smugglers and revenue men but I don't know what you feel about it. I must confess to being a bit deafened by the frequency with which these pop up in every book I have ever read about any coastline from here to Lands End. There is a kind of rubber stamp sameness about them all, like the packages in the supermarket. Anyway, you know where to find them if you want some more. I am going to take you back down the Blackwater, this time having a look at the Southern creeks as we go. If you find them full, incidentally, and decide to anchor off, a riding light is a 'must'.

Lawling Creek and Bradwell

You remember Osea Island, well, half a mile across the river on the south side is Lawling Creek, almost opposite the Doctor when he is on station. (I gather that he took a year's holiday ashore in 1969.) There is a red buoy and once over the bar (three feet LWS) the moorings point the way to Cardnell's boatyard where you will get great courtesy and a few shops, but nothing else. It is a half-tide job except by dinghy, and I think you will have more fun at Bradwell four and a half miles down river where there are a couple of good inns and something to see. The entrance is not easy to spot unless you remember it is about a quarter of a mile south west of the nuclear power station barrier wall. The beacon and first set of withies should be left close to starboard and instead of bothering with the mass of compass bearings sometimes provided by books, use Jack Coote's simple instructions, which even I can understand and run in on echo and the pair of beacons with triangular top marks on Pewit Island, and you should be safe enough following the line of moored craft. If visibility is bad, anchor off and motor in by dinghy. There is good clean landing at the Quay at all states of the tide and you will see *The Green Man* as you round the last bend, standing out by the road with a field between it and the water's edge. But don't be in too much of a hurry, as there are still some muddy humps between you and the door so keep the echo sounder running and watch the withies. There is one visitor's mooring, which suggests early arrival! You can get most of what you want near the quay, including a real 'village shop' with bull's eyes, overhanging windows and a bell that tinkles as you walk in through the stable type door. It used to sell, and I gather still does, candies, paraffin, liquorice allsorts, toothpaste and butter drops in large glass jars.

If you are a masochist or have a yen for a walk of two miles you come to the main village with its old 'lockup' and *Cricketers Inn.* But the real attraction is one of the wonders, not only of Essex but of the whole of the British Isles – a unique Saxon Chapel, St. Peter on the Wall. The Romans first built a fort (Orthona) to hold the Saxons back and the Saxons came and pulled it down and built a chapel across the fort itself as soon as the Roman Empire crumbled. Why it was built by Bishop Cedde in the most ungetatable place in Essex as a gospel headquarters about 654 A.D. no one knows but here it is and it is a gem. Long forgotten and, indeed used as a barn, it has been restored and a service is held here once a year. You can see it when at anchor across the river and now I hope it will stand as long as men continue to remember their past. Certainly the setting hasn't changed much. It stands as it was built on the edge of the marshlands looking over the haunt of the water rail and the ruff, and the shelduck; the marsh wind still moves the tufted hair-grass and clumps of cocksfoot growing along the walls. Their ancestors and the purple moor-grass were there when the Romans came and will remain long after our descendants have forgotten why the simple building was ever cared for and preserved. Perhaps it is better so, for modern man is becoming uncertain of his own right to permanency and when that happens he is apt to lose his way into the future.

Tomorrow we will slip quietly away on the tide up the Wallet; for there is little to attract the sailor between here and the busy port of Harwich, where the remains of Bluff King Harry's Naval shipyard rubs shoulders with the latest and most efficient container docks on the East coast.

Up Coast to Harwich

The passage up the Wallet has nothing to distract the yachtsman from his thoughts and making the best of the wind, which we hope will be the prevailing sou'wester. There is not even anything to see along the shore, that is unless you are a pure masochist and want a nearer view of Clacton Pier and the ungodly sprawl of desirable seaside residences. This has now engulfed Holland-on-Sea, and Frinton is working its way steadily downcoast from the north-east. I firmly believe they were really planned by far-seeing Amenity Societies and Rural Preservation tigers to draw all the lollipop sucking children and plastic carton carriers away from the lovely estuaries where yachtsmen go for peace and quiet – so everybody is happy. This is really why we don't want yacht harbours combined with facilities for tourists when they become available on the East coast. And available they must be, I'm afraid, in the near future if we are to stop estuaries becoming cluttered with moorings, mostly for boats that never go to sea. We must clear them off the fairways so that we can continue to sail in these otherwise enchanting creeks where the wind is constant because there are no high hills to upset the flow.

However, that is in the future, and we are contemplating the present as we make our way up to Harwich, one of the oldest and still most delightful anchorages in the East – not a crowded fishing port like Lowestoft or Yarmouth and with two miles of open water where you may choose your own corner according to the wind, as long as you keep clear of the ferries to Holland and Denmark and the container boats that bustle into Felixstowe on the far side. But while we are covering the twenty miles or so up the coast, I have time to fill in for you the ancestry and background of these people of the creeks so you can see why the fishermen and marsh shepherds remain to this day such a race apart from their slow-moving Anglo-Saxon cousins of the rich hinterland.

There has always been a large admixture of gipsy blood from Tiptree Heath where the smuggled goods were generally auctioned in the seventeenth and eighteenth centuries. The gipsies were so completely involved with the smuggling fraternity of the creeks, that whole generations gave up their wandering life and intermarried freely with the marshmen, leaving behind children with a decided propensity for cunning, hardihood and ruthlessness necessary for survival in a running fight with the establishment in the shape of the Excise men. Then came adverturers, smugglers by trade also, from the Low Countries, France, Spain and even the Mediterranean. They worked the coast with the locals and many stayed for good, bringing a further mixture of blood and Latin temperament to the sluggish muddy blood of the Anglo-Saxon. The Massacre of St. Bartholomew also drove a further lot of Huguenot refugees across. The wealthy went inland and founded the cloth trade, but the more adventurous, or more lazy, stayed in the marshes where life may have been short, brutish and ague-ridden, but money was easy and there were no landed gentry nor hunting parsons to curb their activities. In fact any lesser landowners that were hardy enough to be resident, were equally dependant on the illicit traffic for the few comforts of life. These last immigrants brought not only their Gallic temperament to mixed marriages but an energy and thoroughness in their application to smuggling and farming that has given the marsh area what the wealthy monasteries gave to Suffolk, that is many of its sea walls enclosing vast tracts of what is now meadowland, where formerly mere saltings existed. There was room for all and indeed for nearly a century the Church services in many of the coastal hamlets were conducted alternately in French and English.

The Huguenots infused one more characteristic into the area, the Puritanical bitterness and Calvanistic partiality for the literal adherance to the Old Testament ways and that is why you will still find a large proportion of the children named after Bible prophets and Judaeic warriors, as well as a curious mixture of corrupted foreign surnames, inextricably woven into the basic Anglo-Saxon – all of which goes with the now familiar nasal twang of the talk perpetuated even in Australia by the generations of deported smugglers who were careless enough to get caught and deported if they were lucky. You will hear it among the stagnant pools where the mists lie damp and close and the clouds form in the marsh winds as the sprat boats and the little off-shore trawlers put out for a night's fishing on the Gunfleet. Time has completed the amalgamation of races and they have jelled into something which, you will agree, is quite unique even in this land of hybrids.

Indeed many of the engaging characters you meet today are contradictions which stem from the past. Just this summer I had an enchanting and quite zany conversation with an old friend who runs one of the weather beaten timbered waterside pubs. I had rowed ashore and found him standing in the spring sunshine in his doorway, looking a bit 'other worldly' and with a totally uncharacteristic dreamlike quality about him.

'Hullo Jerry', I said, 'You look a bit pregnant!'

Jeremiah, to give him his full name, regarded me for a moment without seeing me at all, for his thoughts were a long way over the saltings at the end of the street. Then he said, as though he had just come to a momentous conclusion.

'Yeah, it'll be a nice sunny day for it anyway.'

'Yes, I'm sure it will – what for?' I said.

'Yes, I think I'll get him done today. I'd better go and find the Reverend, he's generally somewhere about this time of the day – help yourself, I won't be long.'

'Well, thank you,' I said, 'but why the hurry. Who is going to be done?'

My friend laughed, a little self consciously I thought.

'Oh, just Peter,' (that was his eldest and slightly, shall we say 'avant garde' son.) 'I don't hold much with this religion business, you know but I don't think it'll do 'im much harm and you never know, do you, these days. I look upon it rather as an insurance policy. You needn't worry about it, but, well if things get sticky there it is isn't it.'

It transpired over a pint or two that Peter's confirmation was what was in mind and as Jerry wisely decided that it would be an even better idea if he waited until 'The Reverend' looked in on his lunch-time way to the vicarage, we continued. I said I rather thought there was a little more to it than that.

'I mean you can't just wheel him in and "have him done" at the drop of a hat.'

I remembered a whole series of little chats and much flapdoodle before the event.

'Anyway, where is Peter?'

'Well, that is what I've just thought of. I don't rightly know at this minute. He came in about 3 o'clock last night – this morning – and Maggie says he wasn't in his bedroom come breakfast time.'

I suggest he has a chat with the vicar in slow time, and we leave it at that. As I go back to the dinghy Jerry shakes his head.

'I still don't think it would have done 'im any harm. Still, I'd better find him first.'

And so the East coast goes; it's fun and it's friendly. There is still a bond between all who sail the seas and even in a working community the yachtsman has been accepted as such. Everybody takes a holiday nowadays, even if it's only market day or a weekend in Clacton, so it is assumed the yachtsman is merely a working man, on holiday, and if he takes his holiday battling with the North Sea he is accepted without question into the community.

The Port of Harwich

But the Walton shot tower is abeam and Harwich faint in the haze on the port bow four miles away – Harwich, that magical port where the new and the old blend so unconsciously that it is difficult to trace the passage of time. The waterfront, with its tall Church, esplanade and old Tudor Royal Naval Boatyard shed with the 'Great Wheel' for winding out masts, is ageless and has a fairy-like quality from the water – especially when the morning sun is just lifting the early mists from the jumble of houses, all shapes and sizes. Indeed, time has walked lightly across the town except where the last war bombing removed some of the old timbered streets. But many of the narrow streets and quaint passageways remain with the bow-fronted sweet shops and little fish shops where you can still buy good sea food cheaply and fresh from the offshore trawlers. You can tie up in the Pound, unless it is LWS and slake your thirst at the *Angel,* where Queen Elizabeth landed and now Major Kendall will greet you with good beer and a cheerful fire round which the locals and the customs folk congregate – an old haunt of ours when taking on bonded stores for a three months' cruise in the Baltic or the Biscay Ports. Later you can wander down Church Street and look in at the *Three Cups* – you will be in good company, Nelson and Lady Hamilton used to 'book in' and favoured the room with the Fleur-de-Lys in its Tudor ceiling. Or wander up King's Head Street and enjoy the *Alma* with its pleasant atmosphere and ships in bottles. All trace of the Saxons and Danes who fought over the harbour have gone. but you can come across relics of the time when Drake, Frobisher and Hawkins had more than a noggin in the *Globe* at King's Quay Street or the *New Bell* in Wellington Road before setting out for the Indies and beyond. The Port of Orwell it used to be called; even the ubiquitous *Mayflower* was once registered here and Sam Pepys stood for parliament for the town in the high days of its prosperity in the seventeenth century when fishing was at its best. In 1661 a Packet service to the Low Countries was inaugurated, a forerunner of the train ferry to Zeebrugge which started as a regular service in 1924.

Now in 1972 we have one of the busiest and, so far strike free, container ports on the opposite side of the harbour at Felixstowe. This, with the Dutch and Danish ferry boats, makes cruising in the area constant fun as, what with the stream of Scandinavian timber boats and small tankers using the tide to Ipswich there is always something new to watch – and to avoid when crossing the entrance channel with a fluky wind.

It was here that there was another of the famous Nelson touches. He had come in on the *Medusa* and after a convivial night at the *Three Cups* called for his pilot in the morning to beat out, in case the French arrived on the scene. There was a stinking south easter blowing straight into the harbour entrance and the pilot, wise man, refused to take the unwieldy ship out on a straight beat round the treacherous Cork Sands and Stone Banks. So Nelson promptly grabbed the unfortunate local Marine Surveyor, a gentleman called Spence and said 'we're off'. It was touch and go fairly literally, but they made it safely past the Naze to deeper water and that is why to this day it is called the 'Medusa Channel' on your chart. It is not all beer and skittles in a manoeuverable little yacht and I wouldn't much like to have been in Master Spence's shoes. I bet he got his anchor up at a rate of knots if the tide was showing signs of ebbing.

We cannot leave for the upper Orwell without recalling one of the lighter episodes of the seventeenth century, when the locally built little ship *Fan Fan* took on the whole Dutch fleet anchored outside. It had been a customary sport of young bloods from London to come to Harwich for a nosh up, the excuse being that they were having a couple of days at sea in some naval ship to practise seamanship. On this occasion the party was pretty hectic, one gathers, and there in the morning when the bar-maid upended her customers, was the whole of the Dutch Fleet just outside the harbour. What could be better? Everybody was smarting under the recent disaster at Chatham so the boys stumbled down to the quay where the *Fan Fan* was lying with two toy pop-guns aboard. But let that dashing cavalry officer Prince Rupert, who happened to be on the spot, tell it in his own words – with obviously a length of 'tongue in cheek'.

He wrote to the King on the 27th of July 1666 as follows,

> 'On the previous morning, it being very calm and the enemy to windward, the *Fan Fan*, a small new sloop of two guns built the other day at Harwich, made up with his oars towards the Dutch fleet and drawing both his guns to one side very formally attacked

De Ruyter (in the admiral's ship *Holland*) and continued this honourable engagement so long till she had received two or three shots from him between wind and water, to the great laughter and delight of our fleet, and the indignation and reproach of the enemy.'

One gathers the lads dined out on this ploy for many an evening; perhaps it was just as well that the 'merry monarch' was back in office. I think the austere Cromwell might have failed to be amused.

Old Smugglers' Cottages at the West Mersea on the Blackwater River.

Aerial view of the old town of Maldon on the Blackwater River. *(Photo – Aerofilms)*

The River Orwell

Well, away up the Orwell to Ipswich, the old Saxon Gipeswic, but first a quiet night under Shotley Tower if the wind is in the south west. You will probably be awakened in the morning by the bugles of the Ganges Naval School, but no matter. There is a clean sandy shore – not a common commodity in these parts – and you can anchor in good holding ground close in and well off the buoyed commercial channel to Ipswich docks. Most folk deplore the presence of sea-going commercial traffic but we find it a constant source of interest spotting the ensigns and reading the port of origin on the stern through glasses, because we have sailed into most of them in our own little boat and know them well. Don't be worried if you get a 'roll about' in the middle of the night as one or more go past on the tide, but you need to stow loose objects away the night before to save having to get out of your bunk to collect them off the floor.

Round Collimer Point you come into Butterman's Bay where the old butter-rigged schooners used to lie, bringing coals and general supplies from Newcastle. It has been compared to the Dart, but though the wooded banks are similar, there is much more room to sail and less interruption to the constancy of the wind direction. The pleasant parks of Woolverton and Orwell slope gradually down to the river and occasional little white washed cottages peep out from between the trees on grassy promontories.

Levington Creek

Most people whizz up to Pin Mill, that so called 'Mecca' of East coast yachtsmen, but I would advise you to potter a bit now that you are here. On the starboard side you will see the new yacht harbour where, if you can get in and out without grounding – and I seem to see someone stuck in the dredged channel most times – you can lie to pontoons and have company. But if you want to see Suffolk, pass on to the next

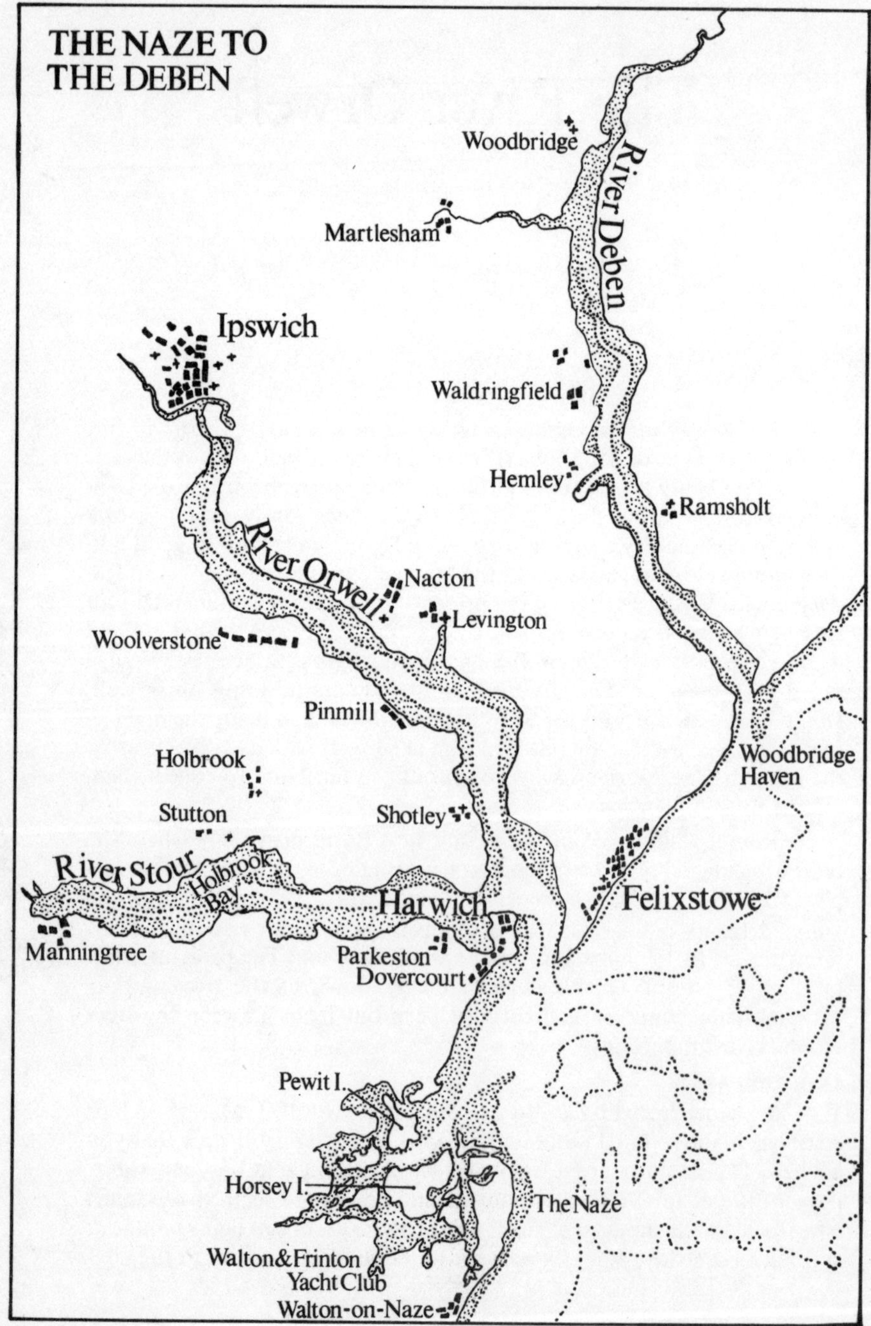
THE NAZE TO THE DEBEN
Woodbridge
River Deben
Martlesham
Ipswich
Waldringfield
Hemley
Ramsholt
River Orwell
Nacton
Levington
Woolverstone
Pinmill
Holbrook
Woodbridge Haven
Stutton
Shotley
River Stour
Holbrook Bay
Harwich
Felixstowe
Manningtree
Parkeston
Dovercourt
Pewit I.
Horsey I.
The Naze
Walton & Frinton Yacht Club
Walton-on-Naze

channel buoy and lead your way up Levington creek if you have legs — or as far as you feel comfortable otherwise, and in that case take the dinghy at high tide to the little wharf at the head. Then in the evening, while your friends sail up and down you can wander a short way into the village to the old world atmosphere of the *Ship Inn,* where the sailormen from the flat-bottomed barges used to come and drink and yarn when they had discharged their cargoes for the surrounding farms.

It is a quiet bit of old Suffolk and still belongs to the river rather than the road and motorised tourist. Back in the main river and just past the old mooring buoys where the lighters used to come down from Ipswich to unload the steamers before the channel was re-dredged, you will see an old wharf by a cottage on the port side, Clamp House hard or in Domesday book, Pringles. Here the peat or turf was stacked for the barges on their return passage to London.

Pin Mill

By this time you will be at the end of a mile or so of moorings and Pin Mill will be opening up on the port side in its charming wooded bay. You can anchor there but unless there is a regatta or meeting I should run on until you are more conveniently near the long low hard. Working from there you hunt around for any yellow mooring buoy. These belong to Jack Ward the Harbour master and if he or his helpful son are not around in the work boat you simply pick it up and ask if it is free when you row in to the *Butt and Oyster* at opening time. You will find Mrs. Ward in the chandlers' shop just behind. It will cost you five shillings, or I should say twenty five new pence, I suppose.

Now, whatever may be said, this is still one of the most enchanting moorings in which to lie afloat. By day there is a coming and going of barges (now privately owned) from the mud flats by the hard and yachtsmen messing about or ships passing round the Potter Point buoy. But best of all is to sit in the cockpit at late evening when the village lights twinkle in a semi-circle and the Great Bear is shuffling round the Pole Star. When all is said and done, where else can you row up to your pub at high water and tie up to the rings in the wall right under the bar window?

There is, of course, the other side of the coin. The shore is very flat and so the gravel and concrete hard is two or three hundred yards long, which is quite a way to carry a dinghy up or down for a long stay. You will see the locals using the little stream at the side and you can often save thirty yards carry by floating it up the brook. Two hours either side of dead low, landing is almost impossible — but, who cares, this is our price for peace and quiet. What shall I say of Pin Mill that would convey even a breath of its charm to those who have never sat at the old bow window of the *Butt and Oyster,* pint in hand and watched the sails go by on the tide or the carpenters working on the old barges high and dry on the shingle spit a few yards away, or walked across the common to the cottages that seem to have been dropped there inconsequentially, as if out of a hat? It has an indefinable charm and even though many of the houses have now passed from local ownership to become the summer snuggeries of new lovers of Suffolk, the general appearance of the anchorage has not changed. The gillyflowers and hollyhocks still grow in profusion nicely wedged in between the vegetable beds; Harry King's boatyard is still as busy as ever and Bob Roberts and less well-known locals still meet in the inn for a 'bit crack' of an evening under our unfailingly cheerful host Peter Watts. The village shop has added chocolate ripple and some more sophisticated sweeties to its range of gob stoppers and other delights and the sailing club opens its hospitable doors to yachtsmen who sail up the river and come ashore to swap yarns.

There is no public car park as such, thank goodness so the motoring hordes soon silt up and leave the rest of the foreshore and hard to sailormen, as it should be. You can fill your water cans at the *Butt and Oyster* after lunch, and I may say the range of food you can take into the bar or eat in the dining room at lunchtime will be an eye opener to most. Next door Mrs. Ward dispenses anything you can think of for your boat, from halfboots to holystones – and where else can you get the latter in these days of plastic decks.

Time was when the coasters unloaded at the lighter buoys in Butterman's Bay and the inn would be full of sailors from distant parts of the world, dancing, singing or just talking and drinking in the ageless camaraderie of sea folk relaxing after a long voyage.

If you want anything the village shop lacks, the mile walk up through the wooded lanes to the village of Chelmondiston – I'm sure it is really called Chumpston! but I've never got anyone to admit to having heard it – will provide an even wider range of goods for the river man.

Woolverstone

Round the next bend in the river – I say this because the yacht moorings are continuous – is the famous old Cat House built in the Regency style with its hard and the refuelling barge of the Woolverstone boatyard. Long ago a white china cat was placed in the lighted window if a run was on, to signify that all was under control ashore. Now-a-days there is a good chandlery and my friend the Chief Engineer who has several times discovered a last minute fault in our diesel just before a long voyage abroad. If you are in trouble over a mooring you climb the steep hill to the little eerie from where Miss Judy Cracknell surveys her forest of moored masts. When you have recovered sufficient breath to speak, and if you talk very nicely to her, she will find you something to tie to for the night. If she can't, even the Archangel Gabriel wouldn't have a cat's chance in hell of doing so.

Diesel, petrol or water you can get without even coming ashore at the end of the gantry by tying up to the floating barge, but, if you are human you will want more than that and across the lawn is the hospitable Royal Harwich Yacht Club where, if you sign the visitor's book, Commander Sterndale-Bennett will see that you are filled up with drink and pointed in the right direction afterwards. Founded in 1843, it is the eighth oldest in the kingdom and backed the first challenger for the America's Cup. Now the Harwich-Hook race is the great event of the year.

Ipswich

It is well worth sailing the remaining four miles or so to Ipswich, past old hards with the delicious names of Pretymans, Nacton, Downham, Mulberry, Middle Dawson's and Greenwich Ness (the oxland of Domesday Book). Fen Bight and Hog Highland have disappeared beneath the modern power station. If you take the trouble to lock in to Ipswich Dock you can do all your shopping and enjoy the variety of motor barges and freighters unloading as they have done since the evil smelling little mediaeval port of Gipeswic developed into one of the busiest ship building ports of Tudor times.

But perhaps you would be in a more receptive mood after a good dinner at the *White Horse Hotel,* still as good as it was in Dickens' day when he wrote of the 'Eat an swill' election or lured Mr. Pickwick into uproarious contact with 'the lady in the yellow curl papers' in this very hostelry, and in 1724 even Defoe found 'very agreeable and improving company almost of every kind.'

The River Stour

Ipswich would fill a book on its own and has done so several times, but I must just take you up the Stour before we look into the Walton Backwaters – those miniature Broads as they are called. The Stour, or Manningtree River as the locals call it, is an odd river. For a couple of miles you sail past lightships brought in for repair, with engaging names like Shipwash, Sunk, Knock John and Dudgeon – poor old Dudgeon always seems to be in trouble. I expect that is why the Admiralty Notices to mariners recently stated rather firmly that their Lordships view with increasing disfavour, if not alarm, the growing practice of yachtsmen interfering with lightships by bringing their yachts into physical contact to the detriment of the light vessel. I wish I could remember the exact wording which was a masterpiece of restraint. The gantries and wharves of the railway docks are less attractive and the Naval Establishment of Ganges opposite is not exactly beautiful. However, once past this lot the river broadens out into a really lovely wooded shallow valley and at first sight it is difficult to see why so few come here to sail.

But the reason becomes clear as soon as you have to decide where to anchor for the night. If the wind is at all fresh and has even a few degrees of east or west in it, there is simply nowhere you can hide from it in any comfort except at Mistley where a promontory shelters you from the west and you can still dry out in about a foot of water and get a meal ashore at the *Thorn,* or a little further on at the *White Hart* at Manningtree. The views from the hill back over the mud flats, at low water, are delightful but it does make you realise another fact, that from Wrabness onwards there is about nine-tenths mud. I rather like mud – in the distance – and the evening lights are just as attractive as on water, after a good meal! There is still a collection of fine old Georgian houses if you poke about a bit and if your imagination fails you, you can remember dear old actor David Garrick looking out of his drawing room window and remarking on 'no less than fifty vessels under sail'. Those were the days of the timber trade to the London Naval shipyards and the 'New Draperies' sent in the sixteenth century by sea as the roads were so bad. Anyway Mistley sent ships to the Armada and had seven regular ships trading along the coast, so there must have been a little more water in those days one supposes.

This was the residence of the famous Matthew Hopkins who was the official 'witch finder general' a practice, one gathers, that had been handed down from father to son rather like a legal practice today. That is until Matthew's operations came to an abrupt end when some bright lad suggested he should undergo one of his own tests. There is Mistley Hall, tucked away behind the warehouses on the quay, of which Horace Walpole once said 'it is the charmingest place by nature and the most trumpery by art, that I have ever seen.' The whole estuary is a bit like that – one moment brilliant with cumulus clouds drifting across the silvery banks and the green woods and the next blotted out by mist or sheeting rain. Perhaps we have been unlucky most times but I do recall some picture nights at anchor off Wrabness half-way down, opposite the magnificent pile – that is the only word for it – of Holbrook where the river is about two miles wide and you can go ashore dry shod in red sand and walk to the village upon the cliff. There is no pub! It is definitely a 'bring your own beer' anchorage. This incidentally is the only anchorage on the East Coast where I have seen great bat-like skate with a wing span of four feet, being speared on the surface by a local fishing boat. It took three men to lift each one in board. I apologise to the Stour if I haven't done justice to it but one can only write of places as one finds them from the water and that has its problems.

The Walton Backwaters

Now we will run through Harwich harbour again with the early morning – well relatively early morning – sun on its old lighthouse and its confidential waterfront and take the tide over the Pye Sands plateau into the Walton Backwaters. I don't care how often I run in here. Like an exciting woman it is always different and always enchanting. But first have a look at your chart and if, when you see the harmless, open bay, you are apt to discount the soundings a bit, just run the Echo a suspicion. There is only about three feet at low water over the Halliday Rock Flats by the Pye End buoy and by Crab Knoll and High Hill the sand banks are very steep-to, though there is thereon plenty of water in the channel – so don't wander about too absent mindedly. I well remember when we were beating in against what had developed into a force six to seven sub gale it was quite interesting, even in an offshore wind. I hate to think of the place in an onshore gale, especially as there are a few rows of old iron spikes on the Dovercourt side, which are not mentioned in any of the 'good books', but the fishermen will tell you all about them.

You can, I know, be too careful. I remember once tacking carefully up to the Horsey Island Point Buoy in a gusty wind with a 'makee learn' at the helm. A little 'whizzbang' speed boat creamed along by us and pulled up in a duther of white water, whereupon a long haired gentleman in a ginger beard leaned out and shouted – 'say mister, wot 'appens if we turn left up 'ere?' Well, I was tempted, but restrained myself and merely said, 'I think you will run out of water.' I thought it rather cut us down to size, in passing!

Stone Point

Now there are two things you can do in the Backwaters: you can enjoy the hospitality of one of the cosiest clubs on the coast or you can anchor far from human habitation in some of the most charmingly desolate little creeks you have ever imagined and listen to the corncrakes and the bullfrogs while you splice the mainbrace in the cockpit at nightfall – that is if you can hear anything above the clamour of the oyster-catchers and gulls on Horsey Island. To take them in turn: the Walton and Frinton yacht club and the shopping centre lies round Stone Point to port as you enter and sail up the Walton Creek. Stone Point, as you will see for yourself is a wonderful place for a bathe as it is another of the sandy beaches and very steep-to. You can run your bow ashore, put an anchor over and pay out a little chain if you wish. But mostly folk anchor off in good holding mud and row a few strokes ashore. On a mild June night when the wind has dropped, I can think of nothing more pleasant than a barbecue ashore. There are plenty of stones for the youngsters to make a fireplace and, as like as not you will find an old iron grill in the bents.

Crab Knoll Buoy

If not, the top of your calor gas stove serves just as well. Over the other side of the grassy hillock you can hear the sea and the shoreline has a wonderful selection of shells for the younger members. Here, as at the Naze cliffs, there are fossils for the picking up; bones of mammoth, aurock, hippopotamus, wild horse, deer and pig have been found – so, have a go. Indeed in one of the streams higher up we used to get that very rare fish, the blue roach but I don't know whether it has managed to survive the march of civilization. Just outside Stone Point there is a swatchway used by the locals, round the coast across Pye Sands keeping about three or four cables off shore but leave an hour or two of rising tide in case of trouble I suggest.

Walton-on-the-Naze

If you want the shops or to sample the hospitable way the steward at the Walton and Frinton Yacht Club welcomes visiting yachtsmen, including delicious sandwiches if you are hungry, (and remember they are the kindly folk who maintain the buoyed channel so it would be a gesture to make a small donation to funds if you use if often) you can run up the Walton Channel through the moorings. But when you come to a fork you will have to make a decision. At one hour and a half before high tide, you can take the left fork and run the last mile right up to the old mill quay outside the club house. There you will find a water tap and fuel after signing in, and repairs at the two boatyards, but you will have to thread your way back through the shallow moorings soon after the turn of the tide unless you have a shallow draught boat. Better turn right handed into the channel delightfully called the Twizzle and pick up any vacant mooring. There is generally someone around to tell you if the owner is away for a few days or likely to be back soon. Then you can motor up in the dinghy to the club, ask about the mooring and pay the boatman at the yard if he says it is all right – you will only be charged the equivalent of 3/6 or possible by now 25 new pence at most. There is water for the dinghy except an hour and a half each side of low but follow the line of moorings or you will be on the mud. There is a hard on the east bank at Foundry Creek but it is a long walk and the better place for dead low water is to land on clean shingle at Colonel's Hard, a few yards up the Twizzle and walk round the sea wall where you can enjoy the wild flowers – if you can shut your eyes to the sprawling caravan park that blots out the hillside.

Walton is a grand shopping centre with wet and dry fish shops and a good spattering of inns.

The Creeks

When you have done your shopping and enjoyed the draught beer and filled the water cans you can unmoor before the evening settles in and hie away to the quiet delights of one of the most unspoilt series of lovely creeks on the East, or for the matter of that, any coast; Arthur Ransome's *Secret Waters,* if you have read that delightful book in your youth. You run back down the Walton Channel and up Hamford Water where there is good wide sailing at all states of the tide. Then you can lie at night between Bramble and Pewit Islands in Oakley Creek on the starboard side, or Kirby Creek round behind Horsey Island or Landermere Creek the far side of Skipper's Island. Horsey Island breeds horses and Skippers is a bird sanctuary, but the birds aren't fussy and are very thick on the ground everywhere. Kirby Creek is our favourite, and though I am afraid there are a few moorings there now-a-days, it is still a peaceful spot with the fields stretching away up the gradual slope to the ancient Church of St. Michael a mile and a half away at Kirby-le-Soken, At high tide, Horsey mere is a great land-locked lake and you can row or motor the dinghy along the withy-marked channel right up to the old Pilot's house at the barge quay. As like as not you will find a barge there as the owner lives on the spot, lucky man. From there it is a pleasant walk to the *Ship Inn* where Miss Pam Reach, the licensee will make you very welcome. You can also land at Beaumont Quay at high water away to the west beyond the little hard at Landermere or you can circle Skipper's Island.

But, why bother if you are in a lazy mood? You are as much away in another and older world with a pipe and a drink at sundown in your own cockpit. Fish flop invitingly round your boat and there is constant activity by the terns, hovering for a moment over a likely spot and then shutting their wings and shooting straight down to the water from sometimes twenty feet up – wham and a big splash. More often than not they seem to come up with nothing visible in their beaks, but they persevere and sooner or later they master the refraction of the water and one more small fish is making his last despairing wriggle in mid air I think this is still a quite unbeatable place for birds, at least the equal of Havergate Island which we shall take you to later on. This wilderness of sedge and sea lavender with its stunted thorn bushes and little clumps of willow and poplar is alive with gulls and oyster-catchers – infact, about this time of evening the noise if often deafening. Teal, mallard, shelduck and shoveller are swooping low over the yacht on their way home to their favourite patches of reed on Horsey Island. You see their wing-tips turn up like miniature aerofoils as they judge their approach and actual landing behind the tussocks. Now and then you see a diver and as you are anchored very near the shore you can see with good binoculars some of the smaller birds, the grasshopper warblers, white throats, chaffinches and sometimes, if you are lucky, a pair of bearded tits. The hordes of busy knots will have gone north to breed but others, like the rare avocets, will be returning to the marshes, though you have a better chance of seeing them a little further up the coast. The greenfinches have a partiality for the low bushes, especially elder and it is about now, in the evening you will hear their gay and elusive little twanging song. Earlier on in the evening with a good pair of field glasses you can watch them building their nests. The first few sticks or fibres are always the great problem and you will see both birds having a shot at getting them in place. There are many failures, then at last two or three stick and the nest becomes progressively easier. The bull finch generally uses fine rootlets and when the rudimentary framework is fixed the hen will get inside and standing almost on her head will push her legs against the lining of the nest. At the same time she will shuffle her body round and round until she is satisfied and has got the walls of her home smooth and fairly regular. Then, when it will withstand wind and stormy weather, she will furnish it with a soft inner lining – often with her own downy feathers.

Shelduck and young

Later in the spring or early summer you can watch the young shelduck scudding about among the sedge at high water like miniature striped torpedo boats – or being taken in line ahead formation across the mud flats at low tide for their four o'clock swim by the proud parents. Often families seem to amalgamate in a sort of 'family minder' system while one lot of parents push off for a bit of a breather down shore. I have seen as many as twenty four being marshalled by one pair. Even when the light leaves the water and hovers with that orange shadow band so delightful in flat country when there is little to break up the reflection, you can still see the black shapes of the stunted thorn bushes against the after glow as the late comers skate over them and fall out of sight. After that the night noises begin and you can have fun guessing the cause of some of the more obvious. You may hear the 'little owl' who likes to build in the scrub willows which fringe the island saltings. He is rather a fine looking gentleman who will often sit in the top of the willow mewing gently rather like a reflective cat.

Anyway, enough of a whiff of this lovely spot, I hope, to give you the flavour of a typical anchorage in the Backwaters. I will leave one last impression with you – the early morning when you potter round the deck in pyjamas just as the sun appears over Horsey mere and begins lifting the mist bands off the water. It is then that the sea birds that have been feeding along the edge of the river in long white bands, rise into the air in great gusts of little bodies. As they turn and wheel against the first light winds they send, from moment to moment, flashes of delicate and rare light from the multitude of their wings; then, as suddenly as the flick of a rapier in the sun or the turning of a diaphanous veil they all wheel together and disappear to the feeding grounds of the day. It is repeated many times as new groups take off. It is part of the age old magic of the saltings which I have never seen equalled, except perhaps, by the great slow moving flights of homing pelicans as they rise from the Hammar Lakes in southern Iraq and turn their silver under-wings into the shimmering light of the desert.

The Deben

It is time to move on, perhaps tomorrow, up country to the Deben (sometimes known as the Woodbridge River) where we have had a mooring for more years than I like to remember. It is best to leave Hamford Water on a rising tide with just enough water to scrape over the plateau and though this means fighting the tide all the way up coast, you will have it to shove you in over the Deben Bar. If you have a really powerful auxiliary of course you can take the ebb up the coast and push in to the Deben over it, but I warn you it runs over the jagged nodules and banks of the underwater ledges at about five knots when it gets going, so you have to do a good six knots to get through the narrows and you have to arrive while there is still sufficient water. Even going up coast remember the water is shallow each side of the channel buoys leading into Harwich, so keep well out from the Felixstowe shore. There is a surface wreck just inside Beach End Buoy and only five feet of water inshore of Platters which is the buoy beyond Rolling Ground. Also there are often fishermen's nets and lobster pots, though these are generally flagged.

The Deben Bar buoy is, of course, changed each time the bar is altered by a severe gale and certainly each spring we look to see where the 'meets' are, on the first passage in or out. These are red and white boards (See Reed's *Nautical Almanac*) and the only problem is that the inshore one is often difficult to see against the row of houses. For this reason it is sometimes replaced by a tall, red, circular openwork marker. One will usually spot the little black bar buoy somewhere under Bawdsey Manor and you can't miss that monstrosity on the cliff. The warning not to come in when there is a strong onshore wind will not need stressing once you have seen the effect it creates. I can assure you it is most unpleasant and can be very dangerous as there are often underwater banks that shoal from fifteen to eight feet almost perpendicularly in some places. In any other winds you should have no trouble. Once in and round the Horse Sands buoy the saltings are flat and not very picturesque for the two and a half miles to Ramsholt but, I think you will agree that the sight of the mooring nestling under its gorse covered cliff above the little Ramsholt Inn and barge quay is one of the pleasantest sights anywhere in the world. So we always think when we have come home from three months abroad.

The Deben Bar in rough weather

I don't know quite how to diagnose the elusive charm of this river – 'The Deep one' as the Norsemen called it when they worked their long boats over the bar and found green woods and pleasant bays to clear for their farmsteadings. Modern yachtsmen or Saxon raiders – they all seem to want to stay once they drop anchor. Now-a-days it is probably a combination of the quiet, unspoilt scenery and the supply of pleasant waterside inns where you can drop anchor just off and row ashore for a pint or a meal and a longer stay if you feel inclined. And four of them are nicely spaced out. First, the old *Ferry Boat* at the entrance opposite

Bawdsey, whose records at least, if not the low ceiling beams, go back to 1181. Fitzgerald, who lived and wrote his Rubaiyat at Woodbridge, was a frequent visitor, with 'Barry' Newson his skipper, both here and at the nearby *Victoria* whose green walls you will spot as you come over the bar. He describes the former as 'an Inn with scarce a table and chair and only bread and cheese to eat', but I can assure you they have both chairs and a pleasant range of 'eats' now.

Ramsholt

The *Ramsholt Arms* itself, formerly the Ferry House and then a farm, is not so old but you will get a warm welcome from Sheila and Eric Smith and you can take your pint out onto the terrace overlooking the whole stretch of river away to the south and the north west. Years back Mrs. Nunn, a great character, would entertain you in her kitchen while you got your own drinks – that is if you were approved of and invited into the privileged circle!

Here in the 'backhus' you would listen to the full flavour of rich unadulterated Suffolk with 'toot' for 'to it' and 'bot' for 'boat' and the 'l' giving place to the 'w' as 'cowd' for 'cold'. There were lovely words like 'grumshus' for obstinate and unbethowt, or somebody described as not having 'a hen's nose full of sense' or, more forcefully, 'about as much sense as t'arse end of a 'hod-me-dod' – a 'hod-me-dod' being the wholly delightful Suffolk name for a snail. Now you have to go further inland for the old 'Suffolk', unless it be the older hands playing dominoes in the *Jolly Sailor* at Orford Quay or the *Anchor* in Woodbridge.

I know the yachting fraternity predominate now but what better substitute could one have in this day and age than the cheerful companionship of those who sail the sea. It breeds a cosiness in the most scratchy of mortals. You cannot sail into Copenhagen or Freetown or the palm girt quays of Basrah or the wooded bays of the West Indies in your own little boat, without hoisting in something of the elemental simplicity of the pure enjoyment of arrival for its own sake. And it is just this that helps to make the cheerful waterside inns of the Deben so attractive. They make a comforting arrival point, not to mention the nightingales that sing to you at Ramsholt and Waldringfield from the little bushes on the cliff as you make your way back to your yacht.

For the mere landsman a new place is generally a means to some business end or at best a scheduled stop in his holiday routine. To the master of a small sailing boat, landfall is an end in itself – the seal of some small bit of navigational achievement, and after days at sea his consciousness is wide open to the simple beauties and wonderment of sights and sounds as he anchors in a strange estuary or alongside a bustling town quay. And he wants to share his enjoyment and talk of difficulties and chance happenings with his fellow man and what better place to

Aerial view of the shoreline at Pin Mill on the River Orwell. *(Photo – Aerofilms)*

The Moot Hall, built in Tudor times at Aldeburgh on the River Ore.

swap yarns than the village waterside pub. This is a great part of the fun of sailing: the fellow in the car in front as you approach your next town is a menace and a contestant for parking space .but the chap on the next mooring, or just dropping anchor astern, is a potential companion of the evening ahead and you wonder what last port he has come from and how he and his crew coped with the dusting you both got during the afternoon when the wind suddenly backed and freshened without warning.

When you are ready you can sail on past numerous quiet anchorages like Hemley where the few farms climb the peaceful slopes and across the river you can watch the busy coming and going in the heronry in the woods beyond the Church above the half mile of delightful sandy beach we call 'The Rocks'. You can anchor off and bathe or look for sharks teeth in the fossil cliffs but let out plenty of scope before you go ashore, as the lower shore has an unfriendly ledge and the holding is a little dicey.

It may be of interest to remember that all the lower part of this river was once the great open port of Goseford, the wool port of the Saxons and where Edward III assembled his fleet for the Calais expedition. The old oval flint Church tower was originally built as a beacon and landmark, and as late as last century the Parish Clerk used to wait until he saw the parson's sails turning the corner from Waldringfield and could assess whether he would make it over the tide, before he rang the bell to summon the congregation.

Waldringfield

On now, round Bowships buoy, the first of the channel buoys, and up to the next cosy inn – the *Maybush* at Waldringfield. Here to port you will see the little sailing club with its figurehead and another sandy beach between it and the *Maybush* perched over the anchorage and surrounded by its pleasant lawn and old apple trees. There is always a permanent gap left in the moorings, just for you and all who care to drop anchor so that you could almost shove the dinghy ashore. Another great advantage is that you are safe from any gale or rough water except, perhaps, the north east which won't often trouble you in the summer. Water you can find at the club or the inn and calor gas and fuel,, while the village shop would put most supermarkets to shame – size for size. Ernie Nunn, if you talk nicely to him – because he is always 'a bit busy' – will patch your boat or sell you bits and pieces from the quayside chandlery. He is still building beautiful boats in wood if you happen to want one.

If you are on the river in August you should not miss one of the most unusual and delightful features of Deben Week, the annual Yachtsmen's Service at Waldringfield. By early afternoon you will see

Yachtsmen searching their lockers for crumpled signal flags, now rarely used except to dress overall on some special occasion. Some are obviously not too certain how to attach and hoist this motley array of bunting, especially as most of us have somewhat incomplete sets of flags which we supplement, not always in the best Naval tradition. But, this is the Deben and the simple aim is to give a cheerful welcome to the Bishop when he arrives from Ramsholt escorted by a flotilla of local boats. Sometimes he comes in one of the more luxurious yachts, dressed overall and with a great St. George's Cross flying proudly from the cross trees; sometimes the honour of bringing him up goes to one of the fishermen at the Ferry in a working boat, but he is always well escorted by dinghies and yachts from every centre on the river.

As the Bishop goes ashore to use the Clubhouse as a Vestry room there is some confusion as the escorting boats try to get themselves anchored as close as possible in a restricted anchorage. By this time the Woodbridge Excelsior Band has arrived and the Waldringfield Parish Church choir while the little beach outside the Club is thick with people. Many more of us do not go ashore, for we can attend the service equally well in our own cockpits. With luck the public address system may even work well enough for us to hear the Bishop's address and we join in all the well known hymns. We do not even miss out on the collection, for the bags are brought round by dinghy while a healthy rendering of 'For those in peril on the seas' floats away down the river.

Now I don't really know what it is about the *Maybush* which draws us to its old bar parlour, high-backed settees and curious ceiling spinner so often when we are back in home waters. Perhaps we still half expect to see those familiar figures Grace and Albert who were gracious hosts to us all for so many long years. They still live in well-earned retirement just up the village street and only this summer we had a 'bit crack' in the Woodbridge wine store. We have been lucky in our 'hosts' of the *Maybush.* Grace has handed over the reins of office to Mrs. Deering who will cook you a magnificent steak in the evening or hot toasted sandwiches for lunch which will do your figure a lot of 'no good' and in the morning you can watch the sun rise over the Ham Woods and wonder why you ever bothered to go all the way to the Danish Islands for a summer cruise. The trees and bushes of the cliff are so close to the steep-to beach that the dawn chorus of land birds drowns even the oystercatchers and knocks six bells out of a still spring morning.

Next day as you nose your way carefully up past the Tips and negotiate Troublesome Reach – never was a reach more appropriately named you will think as you go aground – past buoys with lovely names like Jack Rush and Crummy Moore and Methersgate Quay, you can think of the old Saxon ships hurrying past for the great burial at Sutton Hoo above you on the west shore or enchanting figures like Edward Fitzgerald drifting down with his boatman buddy, 'Pork' Fletcher, dressed generally in any old clothes that came to hand and a dilapidated old stove pipe hat on his head. His pockets were stuffed with lollipops and sticky sweets for the crowd of adoring children that collected outside each pub as he put ashore. Tennyson, Carlyle, Crabbe and the literary stars of the day all came to see and to talk to this strange withdrawn man. He took them all in in his own dreamlike way, but always he was happiest in his little boat pottering from inn to inn and often over the bar up coast to the Alde where we will follow him as soon as we have shown you Woodbridge. He was a strange mortal, some say over conscious of the impermanence of our life. They remember always

'And, as the cock crew, those who stood before
The tavern shouted, 'open then the Door!
You know how little while we have to stay
And, once departed, may return no more!'

Or they will quote to you,

'Yon rising moon that looks for us again –
Through this same garden – and for one in vain!'

And that is all they remember about one of the most delightful characters our river has known. I got to know him more intimately I think through the sensitive charm of his early poetry. Here is a passing verse from an old notebook when he was a student:

'So winter passeth
like a long sleep
From autumn fall
to primrose-peep!'

That is the real man I think of as I sail up to Kyson below his home town of Woodbridge. In spring time I always have a soft spot for the little pink rose with the feathery leaves in my own garden, whose ancestor, now called Omar Khayam, was brought all the way from the Persian poet's grave and planted on Fitzgerald's when he died in 1898. It is rather a pleasant, inconsequential little bloom – not unlike the poet himself.

Woodbridge

You can lie in six feet of water off the wooded headland of Kyson and see the little town of Woodbridge spread out round the square tower of St. Mary's Church in the sunshine; it is a pleasant walk along the bank from the land or twenty minutes in the dinghy to the town hard. The other way is to come and go on the tide or tie up in the old mill harbour just after half-tide, where George Whisstock's harbour master will look after you and you can walk ashore from a dry pontoon with fuel, water and all supplies on the spot. You will have heard of the Tide Mill, the last to remain working and now in need of funds to prop it up. But of Woodbridge, one of the most enchanting old county towns you will ever wander round, how can I do it justice in a few words? You will have to read *Suffolk Estuary*. If you ask my friend Mrs. Barbara Hopkinson in the Deben bookshop in the Thoroughfare, she will produce it for you, complete with the Woodbridge Mariner on the dustjacket – for, of course, the exchange of a few bawbees.

The Market Square at Woodbridge

Woodbridge also, is a place of ghosts – ghosts of the old coasting brigs that were built here to take Suffolk timber to the Thames Naval ship-building yards and coal from the North – ships that is, of up to four hundred tons were launched and maintained here until the river silted up. These were replaced early in the last century by faster, cheaper schooners; faster because fore and aft rig had supplanted the clumsy square-sails. Then came the 'Billy boys' and 'boomies' and a host of other types of sea-going barges until this twentieth century has seen the four remaining boatyards concentrating on yachts like the beautiful wooden carvel fifteen tonners still being turned out at the Whisstock yard where we lay up Kala Sona in the winter or the modern GRP boats being fitted

The Ore

The little bar buoy had lost its top last time we saw it but it is of no consequence as you probably won't find it anyway until long after you have spotted the leading marks on the shore – 'meets' as they are called for obvious reasons. They are much more easily seen than those on the Deben entrance as there are no buildings anywhere near to confuse you – white boards against the dark brown of the woods. Keep a good mile offshore as the semi-circle of shoals runs far out and then keep the meets carefully in line as you run in past the bar buoy. When you are a cricket pitch from the shore line below the markers you can safely turn to starboard into the river mouth.

It is a queer place this river Ore, which higher up becomes the Alde; you sail up it for ten miles and you are still less than a hundred yards from the open sea. In medieval times the port of Aldeburgh was to the north of the town; then nature and the gales took it in hand and having wiped out two-thirds of the little town, spread a ridge of shingle down to Orford, which became the sea port of early Tudor times, after which time the 'build-up' continued for three or four miles to Shingle Street where the entrance now is. Long Reach is nearly straight as far as Dove Point on the end of Havergate Island, and as the tide swishes you up it like an express train, you can enjoy the sea birds paddling about the type of landscape that hasn't altered since long before Julius Caesar was dropped into his first toddling clothes. It is the land of smugglers, shepherds, fishing smacks and the marshland farmers. If you want to get the flavour of it as recently as the beginning of last century, you have only to read that legendary, but true, story of Margaret Catchpole, or give anyone in Suffolk a pint of beer and it will pour out while you wait. She was a quite exasperating serving wench who fell in love with Will Laud, a smuggler. She spent most of her time hiding goodies to take to him, that is when she wasn't either going to prison herself or escaping from an upstairs prison window or doing a John Gilpin on a 'borrowed' horse all the way to London. Eventually her Will got shot escorting her to a lugger waiting off this shingle bank, whereupon after yet another trial she was finally and this time successfully deported to Australia on a convict ship. But she wasn't done yet, the air seemed to suit her and she had another twenty nine pleasant years happily married to the brother of the Excise man who had shot her lover. By this time she was full of good works and had a large tombstone erected to her in Sydney by a host of grateful followers – quite a girl in her way.

In fact, to the old gossips in the marshland inns she has never really died; only this summer an old crony with whom I was discussing a point or two offered to show me the entrance in the cellar of his own flint cottage, to the tunnel she and Will had used to the shore on that fateful morning. He became particularly lyrical during the next few pints but when we tottered off to see it, he found that his niece had gone shopping in Alderton and wisely turned the key in the door to make sure he had no excuse for not finishing his jobs in the garden. Perhaps it turned out for the best.

Havergate Island and Dowsing Island are now one piece of desolate land where the wind soughs in the bents and you may see that delightful little bird the avocet, which has again been induced to breed here after many years' absence. You can anchor off the shore in Abraham's Bosom or any of the other quiet bays and enjoy them through your binoculars. The little, red house of the shepherd who used to attend the sheep and signal the 'all clear' as necessary, has long since crumbled into the general desolation, but it is a grand place for his friendly little ghost to wander on misty nights when it is easy to imagine almost anything moving around the dark shadows of the bog pools. Abraham's Bosom was so named, according to Mr. Arnott because there is an abundance of good soles! I don't trust myself to comment on that, but I am sure he would know.

This is another river on which you can find something to suit every mood – pubs and good company in Orford and Aldeburgh, not to mention home-smoked salmon, oysters, and smoked sprats you can take back aboard for breakfast – and at Iken or in the Butley Creek you can find a peace and other worldliness that you would have to travel now-a-days to the outer Hebrides to equal.

The Butley River

We will turn into the Butley River first as we are already at the entrance. This is difficult to find at the end of the Lower Gull but as you turn right-handed into the Upper Gull and look back, there it is. Be careful of the long mud spit to port as you run in. On the right you have the Gedgrave Marshes and over the seaward bank on the left lie the lonely stretches of the Boyton Marshes. There is plenty of water as far as Boyton Dock, where the barges loaded the farm produce before roads were metalled, for the deepest draught yacht to swing happily at LWS and you can land from a dinghy at the dock even at low water.

Avocets

What is the attraction? I think it is more than just the peace and quiet after the bustle of busy moorings. When I think of this river, I think of sheep grazing on the hills and the marsh tracks, of miles of sea lavender in full bloom alongside the marsh samphire and sea astors and of a bewildering variety of waders along the shores that have no fear of man as long as he is floating peacefully on a boat at the end of a chain. Nowhere can you enjoy such complete silence. I mean cessation of man-made noises because for me bird song is an integral part of a country silence that is in reality made up of a number of little noises if you have the patience and understanding to trace and assimilate them.

This is a land as laboriously reclaimed from the North Sea as any in Holland. The Normans started it and the Austin Canons of Butley

Priory took over as soon as they had established their little quay for unloading stone for the buildings. Indeed they pursued it with such energy, using doubtless threats of hellfire and damnation to all locals refusing their labour, that by 1500 most of the sea walls you can see from your yacht had been built and the saltings transformed into the meadows where dreamy-eyed cows and horses weigh you up with a contented stare as you go by on your way from Boyton Dock to the cheerful little inn. The walk up to Dock Farm is wholly delightful when the wild flowers are out along the ditches and the toadflax, bugloss, hound's tongue, dittander, scentless mayweed, wild chamomile, hemp nettles and above all, the old fashioned poppies are at their best. You will get a pleasant welcome at the *Bell* at Boyton and good beer and ham or cheese sandwiches, along with friendly talk with the locals if you are in the mood for it. It is a real village inn where the villagers meet and discuss the affairs of the day while the youngsters play darts as it is off the main roads and tourists are not encouraged – except, that is, folk like yourself who arrive the right way, by sea, and take the trouble to walk up from the creek. The village is not spectacular, the Church of St. Andrew isn't old, except the Norman doorway of the vestry, but the reconstruction fits in and the alms-houses are fun. It is a typical Suffolk village where heath and marshland meet and the cottages are comfortable rather than picturesque. Anyway it makes a good excuse for half an hour's walk and the good lady at the village shop is most obliging and quite inventive. They used to export clay to Delft and Chelsea for pottery manufacture – I don't wonder, when you have scraped a few lots off your half boots down in the creek you may wonder why they bothered to glaze it.

Personally, having a shallow draught boat with a centreboard we tend to gravitate to our own mooring, allowed by the kindly landowner, round the corner up under Gedgrave Cliff just below Mr. Spinney's oysterage. The outlook from the cockpit on a warm summer's evening is pure delight. There is not a habitation in sight and, unless the American army of occupation at Bentwaters is making the air hideous doing circuits and bumps, only the bleeting of the sheep as they wander in line astern over Barrow Hill as the sun goes down behind it. It is then one gets to speculating on the past when the hill was a Bronze Age stronghold, dominating the creeks and coastal waterways until the Romans came and organised everything into a dull pattern of standard behaviour. But you can't organise Suffolk and even the Romans gave up the unequal struggle after 400 years, leaving the field clear for Saxon and Dane to battle it out. I think it is these old ghosts that dominate the landscape when the great cumulus cloud shadows chase each other across the dykes and water of the little Tang River that runs inland from the hard. When the old Norse raiders were finally pushed back into the sea, they left behind old gods, Gods you can so easily feel in this lonely spot, brooding over the saltings. The present day legends of 'Black Shuck' the phantom dog the size of a calf and with fiery eyes must surely be a descendant of Garm the hound of Odin who, as you must know, swallows the moon at the time of its eclipse.

During the late evening afterglow, you will see the night heron, a rare bird I have not spotted anywhere else, fishing opposite Gedgrave Cliff. There are mallard, teal, shelduck, snipe and coot and sometimes you will hear, rather than see, the wing beats of the great grey goose – 'Gabriels Hounds' as they are called in Suffolk, homing to the saltings for the night. Their feathers kept our bowmen's shafts straight and true at Agincourt and Crecy and they were locally supposed to fly only on the eve of some coming disaster. But that was all long ago. Now, as you snug down for the night or stretch your legs along the sea wall you can see the friendly lights of Orfordness, the Cork, Sunk and Shipwash lightships and the loom of the Outer Gabbard lighting peaceful sailor men to harbour or giving them a compass reference on their way out to distant lands.

Orford

Now for a change, you could do a lot worse next day than drop anchor in the fairway off Orford Quay for lunch. Keep well downstream of it as the ferry to the Ministry establishment opposite uses the upper side and you'll have some rude words if you block the channel. On the way up the Upper Gull past Havergate Island – another pleasant night's anchorage by the way – have the binoculars ready as, besides avocets there is a goodly range of wildlife. Only this year we have logged down sitings of whimbrel, bar-tailed as well as black-tailed godwits, lesser yellowlegs, curlew sandpipers, little ringed plovers and turnstones, as well as a host of more usual fellows between Butley and Cuckold's Point – lovely name. Round this last point you will see Orford Quay nestling beneath the castle and its Church (which always seems to be in need of patching) and alongside the old custom house and red roofs of the riverside cottages.

Orford is an old village you will find yourself returning to time and time again, whether it be to the long wooden settees of the *Jolly Sailor* where Sidney Harber, like his father before him, used to open oysters for you, washed down with good draught Guinness while Mr. George Brinkley and his friends played dominoes with verve and cunning and the talk was in broad Suffolk dialect not only of mooring problems but of the great days of the cod smacks and sprat boats. Sprats are still one of the staple industries and further up the street left-handed on to the village square you can still have the most deli-

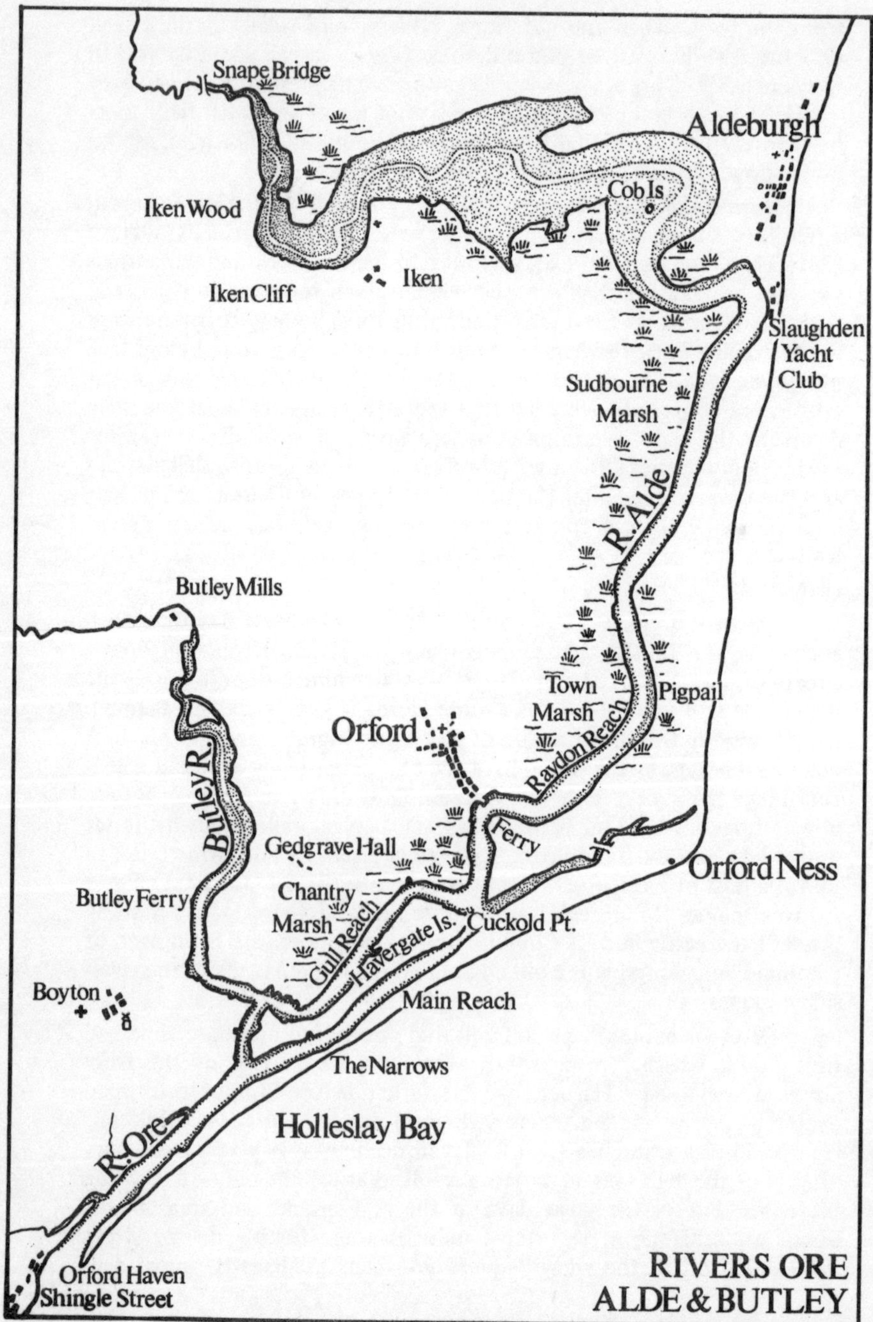
Snape Bridge
Aldeburgh
Cob Is
Iken Wood
Iken
Iken Cliff
Slaughden
Yacht
Club
Sudbourne
Marsh
R. Alde
Butley Mills
Town
Marsh
Pigpail
Orford
Raydon Reach
Butley R.
Ferry
Gedgrave Hall
Orford Ness
Chantry
Marsh
Butley Ferry
Cuckold Pt.
Gull Reach
Havergate Is.
Boyton
Main Reach
The Narrows
Holleslay Bay
R. Ore
Orford Haven
Shingle Street
RIVERS ORE
ALDE & BUTLEY

cious plates of locally smoked salmon, herrings and buckling you have ever dreamed of. This is at the *Butley Oysterage,* which is now licensed so you needn't bring pints of beer across from the *King's Head,* as we used to do.

The smoking is done down at the actual Oysterage and the helpings are generous – only here have I eaten about as much smoked salmon as I could manage at a sitting and all for 75 pence. Afterwards you can take a bag of smoked sprats or mackerel back aboard for breakfast next day. The *King's Head* also has a jolly good snack bar and a rather expensive range of wines. The back of the pub is in the church-yard and nowhere else that I know, does a brewer's dray have to back up among the tombstones to deliver its load of beer. There is also the *Crown & Castle* where you can enjoy a good dinner in the peaceful atmosphere of the 'well-to-do'. The castle itself is a bit 'curate's eggy', fun in bits with a jolly good view of the estuary from the roof.

One hint, don't choose a day with a strong wind over tide, as tide runs fast past Orford Quay and you will get very, very wet in the dinghy as you come ashore. It can't have been much wetter in Tudor times when Orford was a sea port before the shingle bank shut it in and took the entrance five miles down the coast where we came in. There were revenue cutters based here in which men with the curious title of 'boat sitters' were paid a shilling a time to con the craft when in pursuit of smugglers.

The Alde and Slaughden

The way ahead up to Aldeburgh by the back door at Slaughden Quay lies past another series of delightful old names for the reaches and little bays. I am afraid there is also a monstrous array of aeriel knitting on the ministry side but this can't be helped and, indeed, in some lights it is almost impressive. If you can 'lay' down Raydon Reach, past the old farm which takes its name from the rye grass which still grows in such profusion, you can 'lay the main', the locals will tell you. Then comes Pig Pail, Black Stakes with its Brick Bars and on to Lower Dan's Hole, called after old Dan Winter who lived in a cottage on the marsh and was a bit of a local character. Then at the end of Aldeburgh Long Reach where the Ore becomes the Alde you see the town, or rather the end of it as we are using the back door, with its old barge residences, yacht club and disused lighthouse. It looks good on a sunny day and you anchor conveniently just short of the obvious yacht club hard. This is an easy place to land provided you do the secretary the courtesy of calling on him and asking if you may sign the visitors' book. You will find them friendly folk and they have recently gone all modern and organised a telephone so if you are lazy and don't feel like a mile walk to the *Cross Keys* and back with a load of shopping, you can call a cab.

Just one vital bit of advice; this is the only place on the whole river where you can get piped water straight into your tank so don't miss the opportunity, especially if you are going on to the wilds of Iken for the next night as I propose. This you can only do at about two hours either side of high water depending on your draught, so look at the tide tables before pottering off to the town and, as my friend Freddy Cane is kind enough to lay this on for you as well as supplying the hose, he will appreciate a couple of bob left on the water cock stand when you have re-coiled the hose! I am sure you will meet 'Jumbo' Ward, who still pilots the barges through the twisty upper reaches of mud and reeds to Snape and as he has announced his retirement from his usual full activity he may have a moment to tell you of the old days at Slaughden, when it was a busy port with two inns including the *Three Mariners*. Indeed at the turn of the century there were eight habitations at Slaughden including boatyards that built the Aldeburgh cod smacks. Then the sea washed them away and now even the cosy bar of the *Three Mariners* with its whale bone over the door has gone with the rest of the cottages – away down coast to join the shingle and debris pounded by the implacable North Sea waves, which have already taken three-quarters of Aldeburgh itself. What a pity we can't still wander up from the old quay and wrap ourselves round a noggin or two on the spot before facing the walk to Aldeburgh.

There is nothing there now except the Martello tower with its thirteen foot thick walls, and the new Yacht Club and the boatmen's tarred huts leading down to the wooden quay. Anyway 'Jumbo' is still there, complete with gold earrings, putting the younger generation through their paces in his little sail boat or organising the matters of lay up and fitting out. Time was, as I well remember, he would meet your yacht in midstream and point out a mooring as he gave you a card of welcome from the yacht club and if you didn't luff-up neatly enough for his critical eye you got a free lesson in the art – in broad crisp Suffolk!

Aldeburgh

Ah well, I hope you will walk into Aldeburgh and see it for yourself because, now that I come to tell you why you should go there I find it difficult to know where to start – perhaps with the banks of hollyhocks and hydrangeas of all colours, that light your way in past the enchanting old Custom's House and seaward cottages of all shapes and combinations of soft red brick and decorative flint.

I think it is in just this absence of any pretence of being grand or sophisticated or 'with it', that the real charm lies. There is an unhurried atmosphere of more leisured ages about its narrow streets and truncated waterfront. Summer visitors and yachtsmen meander in and out of its little shops and mingle happily in its old inns. The magic of an older world hangs about the haze of summer evenings until the street lights bring the cobbled alleys into perspective and lighted windows on the pavements fill the air with the smell of fresh herrings being fried in butter.

The Old Customs House at Aldeburgh

At the *Cross Keys* behind the lifeboat station you may solace yourself with good bitter and Butley smoked salmon or platters of fresh seafood as you sit in the sun on wind-bleached benches in the backyard or, if it is a bit parky, in the eighteenth century comfort of the enlarged bar parlour. Or there is the *Commercial,* now called the *East Suffolk Arms,* on the broad High Street, to mention only two of the many surviving hostelries that still open their hospitable doors.

I mustn't on the other hand give the impression that Aldeburgh has always been a quiet place. It is only taking a rest after a very strenuous past. It is still very conscious of the Elizabethan days when three hundred sprat boats sailed up for the 'Spratte Fare' or a hundred fishermen launched their little cockboats down the seaward shingle on greased rollers as their descendants still do when the weather allows. There is a whole book in itself from a reading of the lifeboat records on the station or the records of local boats in the wills of long since departed inhabitants. The old Moot Hall, once in the middle of the town square, now stands gaunt and forbidding on the beach, just as it did when Frobisher was locked up in it for an act of piracy and only released when he indignantly demanded his freedom to ride to Queen Elizabeth's Court to petition for his own release. Soon, the waves of the North Sea will claim this Tudor gem as they have already claimed so much of the old town itself. Aldeburgh ships have fought and foundered in most corners of the Empire, but perhaps the spirit of the free fishers of the East coast is best recalled in the local song of the 'Aldeburgh Cod Bangers' that you used to hear as the high spirited youngsters swaggered down Harwich waterfront or Aldeburgh High after a successful spell at sea:

'When we come to Harwich Pier
The folks all flock from far and near
To see us heave our cod on deck
And smack 'em on the head with a Bloody great stick'

They were a tough, weatherbeaten lot, fearing neither God nor devil nor the elements, but perhaps a little shy of anything that smacked of discipline – a legacy from the old smuggling days. The touch I like as well as any comes from George Carter who recalls during the last war a well intentioned naval Commander suitably impressing some new personnel the first night aboard his ship with the admonition

'My men, you are in the Navy now, and in the Navy we tame *lions!'* The effect of this stern opening note was a bit shattered by a cheerful Aldeburgh erk who piped up in broad Suffolk,

'Lor' bless 'e sur, that's nawthin, back 'ome in Aldeboro, we eats the buggers!'

The Way Up to Iken

On that happy note let us return to the anchorage and in the morning make sail for Iken and the now legendary Festival Hall in the old Maltings at Snape. This, with Butley, is the other most beautiful anchorage on this or any river. First though, there is some tricky pilotage to be done and on a rising tide at that, so that you arrive about an hour before high in case you clot it and hit the mud.

There are, I had better warn you, some forty withies to negociate. 'Jumbo' used to put tomato tins on the port withies and some bits of black cloth, from what female relative's undergarments I don't know, to indicate those to starboard. Up West Row Reach you go away inland from the sea at last, and on round to Cob Island into the broad shallow waters of Blackthorn Reach with the sloping shore a bit pock-marked now by bijoux residences which are well away in the distance, so no matter. Up Collier's Hall Reach, so called after the Snape coal barges, past Charlie Ward's beacon to port, marking the favourite 'hitch up' of the old wild fowler and the two kettle beacons, kettle meaning fish basket traps in the old days and a lot of other withies with delightful local names like Lonely Anne.

My advice, engendered of bitter experience, is to count the withies carefully because as the channel wanders about so aimlessly, especially in the lower and upper Troublesome Reaches, it is quite easy to miss a sharp turn of almost a hundred and eighty degrees and make for a much nearer pair, which are actually two bends away with a shallow mud ridge between you and them. That is why a rising tide saves a lot of temper and frustration unless you carry legs and can play bridge until the next tide floats you off again. I know one hopes to be smart enough to back the foresail or kedge her off, but it depends a bit where the wind is and, brother, can this mud cling!

The Oaks

Anyway, when you have done the last two S bends successfully across to the Church and out again you will see four large oak trees just as you turn to starboard below Iken Cliff. We always drop here as there are now too many moorings under the cliff itself and this is far more lovely as you look right across the stretch of water to Black Heath wood a mile and a half away with St. Botolph's Church standing out on its rocky promontory. It is shallow, only about three feet of water at LWS, but the mud is very soft and you will hardly go over; at neaps there is always sufficient depth. The shore is sandy and a grand picnic place for the kiddywinks while you have a ziz or wander off to the village pub about a mile away.

The sea birds are a joy, just as they were in the Butley with perhaps a greater number of dunlin, turnstones, stint and terns mixed in with the usual curlew and oyster-catchers. The grassy bank beyond the sandy beach is greatly indented between the tussocks and here you will see another favourite Suffolk pastime going on at weekends and holidays – eel-pritching. If you look closely when the tide has receded you will often see two small holes, these will in all probability be eel blow-holes. It is between these that the locals probe about with their fearsome looking fan shaped barbed hooks facing inwards until some poor eel is firmly wedged between two barbs. Then he is put in a bag and secured, as they can travel long distances if dropped on land. The other method

I have seen both here and on the Continent is, of course, the eel net beloved of Ijsselmeer fishermen. Old and young, they come and prod the banks or sit patiently over their nets until dusk when they trail home and leave the haven to you and silence in the half luminous dusk that one always associates with the saltings. They say herring and even salmon trout still come up as far as Iken and roach come down stream from Snape but I can't vouch for this as we don't seem to have much luck fishing from the yacht.

The Quay at the Maltings with barge unloading

In the old days, barges stopped here to load sand as ballast for the home run down the coast. Now the few that struggle up to Snape, come back with a load of gear for the Ministry site opposite Orford. They don't come often but I should ask at Aldeburgh whether any are expected before you go off at high tide leaving your yacht anchored in the middle of the fairway; barges in a hurry are apt to be a little careless! You are safe enough except at high tide and in the middle of the narrow fairway. There is a pleasant village pub about a mile's walk away but I expect you will be doing as we do and motoring up in the dinghy to the *Plough and Sail* at Snape – you have to shop there anyway.

Now this is not a chore, it is one of the most delightful mile and a half runs of twisting channel through primeval reeds and little creeks that I know. You can take your yacht up and dry out, by permission, against the Malting's quay, just as the barges do but if you make a nonsense of any of the winding, twisting bends you may have an uncomfortable night instead of the pleasant company in an inn. In any case you can enjoy the waders and occasional avocet among the tall reeds that cannot have changed since ancient Bronze Age man dug, drank and was buried among the gorse hillocks of the landward slopes. Often we have stayed longer than we meant in the little pub and had to grope our way by moonlight from Wolf's Hole, withy to withy, down upper and lower Broad Point to Tom Totty Beacon. In the *Plough and Sail* you will still hear the expression 'up tack and down peak and wear her round Tom Totty'.

Snape

As you round the last corner you see the rebuilt Festival Hall behind the Maltings Quay to port with possibly a barge or smaller craft loading. But, I'm afraid you will no longer see the old Snape Bridge in front as it has been replaced by a new one, pleasant enough but a bit twentieth century functional. The old hump-backed narrow bridge was a gem and was maintained by Aldeburgh town council which depended on it as the lowest crossing of the Alde. It was as famous as the Martlesham Lion, indeed according to George Arnott, there is a very old map painted on a gallery wall in the Vatican in Rome and illuminated in gold-leaf brought back by Columbus from the New World. It is a map of the world and naturally at that time most of the space is filled by 'Terra Incognita' as you would expect. But England is shown with only two places named – Walsingham and Snape Bridge. A pilgrim's way perhaps? Or was it drawn by yet another wandering Suffolk cartographer who just couldn't resist marking his home village out of pure nostalgia. How human and cosy; I well remember when I was a serving Officer in the Desert. the first thing British troops did after establishing a new R.A.F. Station was to erect a signpost on the mud road outside which read maybe Baghdad ten miles, Khadimain so many more, but always London 3,479½ or whatever it happened to be.

The *Plough and Sail* has been modernised outside and now has an annex catering for Festival audiences but the old bar parlour is still there with its semicircular highbacked pine settee and scrubbed tables. There is an old story that the bargemen used to plant barley in the cracks of the table and water the grains with beer, promising to come back later for the harvest. But I presume the proprietress removed the shoots as they came up; anyway, I am sure you won't find any now in the clean atmosphere of the present establishment. The shops are half a mile away at Snape Street, where the marshland meets the green fields of the hillside. You walk past banks of wild mallow set among the ragwort, shepherd's purse and cow parsley. You will find all you want for the next few days' cruising, what with modern cold storage added to normal village shop universality, and the old *Crown Inn,* amongst several, is worth a visit if you are still thirsty, with its black rafters, beams and trapdoors. It has a sort of indifferent air of more leisurely and ancient times, as if it wouldn't really notice if the village disappeared in a whirlwind but would carry on serving drinks to anyone left over from the cataclysm.

From Shingle Street to Southwold

Well this is about as far as you can go, unless you row the dinghy up to Little Glemham and Farnham, so back round the twists with a nod to old Tom Totty and next day all of twenty-one miles back to the bar at Shingle Street for the passage up coast to Southwold. It is always rather good to feel your boat come alive again after days in a river, however attractive it may be, and come alive it will if the wind is anywhere between north and south west so listen to the weatherman at 06.45 hours before pushing through the white waters over the bar.

When the time comes to run out over the bar (though I realise you will have to go out with the ebb if you have no auxiliary) I strongly advise you, assuming an average motor, which will push you about five knots, to go out against the make, leaving just before half tide when there should be plenty of water. If you hit anything you will only be doing about a knot over the ground, but with the ebb you go out like a cork from a champagne bottle and if you are unlucky enough to hit a rock-like shingle nodule at ten to eleven knots, you will probably leave your keel behind as a parting gift.

Having got safely out and beyond the bar, you have no problem except to avoid the Whiting Bank to starboard and, round Orfordness to run up the coast outside the Dunwich Bank, because both banks can kick up very nasty seas in certain winds. You don't fool around twice with East coast shoal banks; some like the Shipwash, drop seventy feet sheer into a ravine – no wonder the chart says, with a penchant for understatement 'Strong Ripples'. I must say Aldeburgh, sliced off though it is, always looks rather good from the sea. I expect that it is partly that we are so used to seeing the old lady's backside from the river that we forget she is quite a 'sweater girl' eyeful round the other side. You will also recognise Thorpeness and then five or six miles beyond, you can just spot a wee village in a few trees on the cliff top and the remains

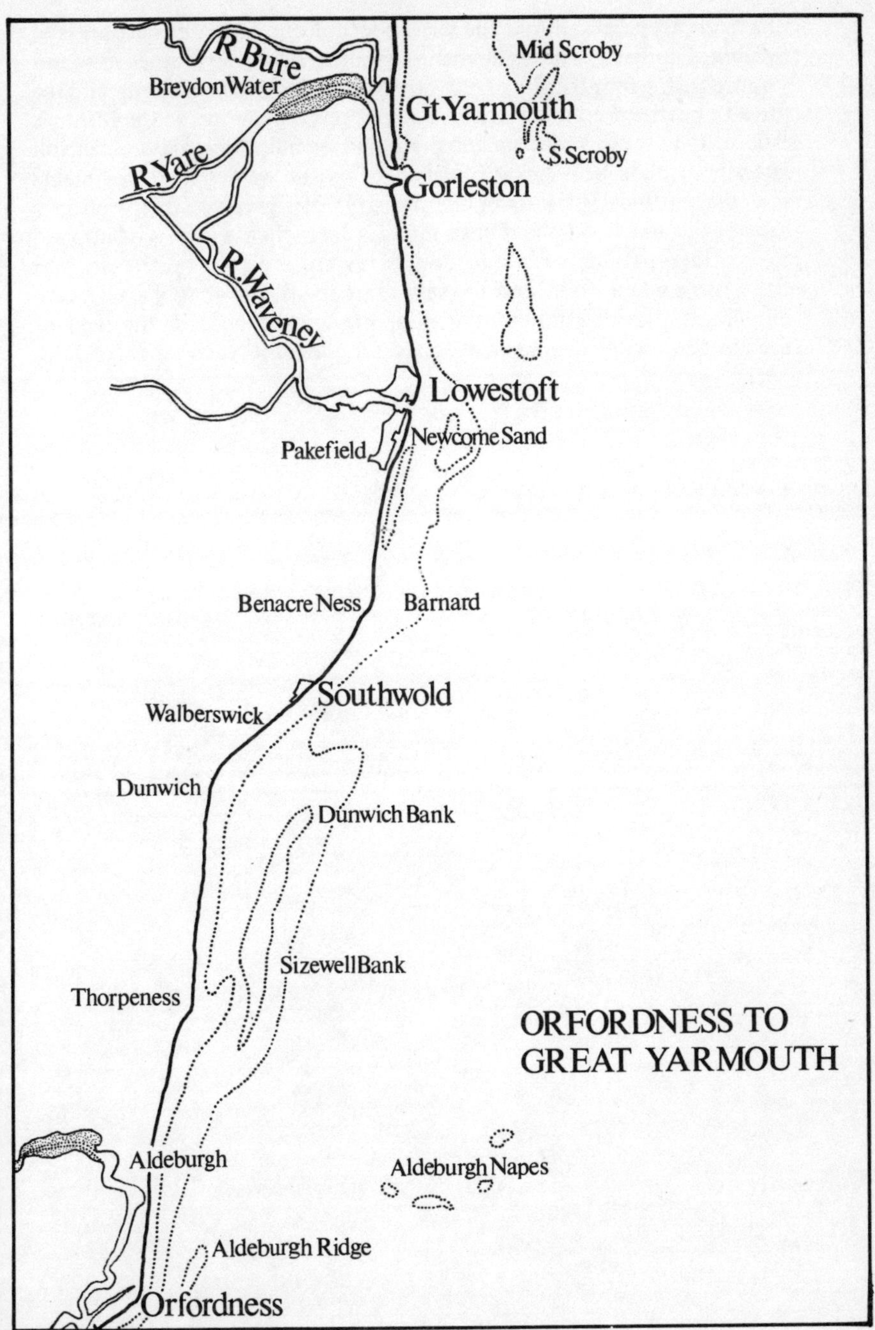
R.Bure
Mid Scroby
Breydon Water
Gt.Yarmouth
S.Scroby
R.Yare
Gorleston
R.Waveney
Lowestoft
Newcome Sand
Pakefield
Benacre Ness
Barnard
Southwold
Walberswick
Dunwich
Dunwich Bank
Sizewell Bank
Thorpeness
ORFORDNESS TO
GREAT YARMOUTH
Aldeburgh
Aldeburgh Napes
Aldeburgh Ridge
Orfordness

of a monastery. It is all that the sea has left of one of the busiest ports in Suffolk, Dunwich. The few remaining cottages are very quiet now and you are sailing over the site of old timbered houses, town gardens and the life and bustle of cobbled streets leading to the quayside or the Bishop's Palace. If you are a glutton for myth and legend, they say you can still hear the broken bells being rolled about by the waves on stormy nights like the mythical Atlantis or the last days of Lyonesse. But what gets me are the much simpler things that are lost when a city is destroyed, the cottage parlour with somebody's favourite corner by the fire and the taverns where folk used to meet after the day's work. Palaces can be rebuilt but the kindly things of life survive only in the land of dreams and half remembered songs sung by the sailor men of later years.

Southwold

The red roofs and great white lighthouse of Southwold are already in sight and as you will have realised from your charts and pilot books, the entrance is a good mile before the town – now-a-days up the river Blyth by Walberswick in fact, with its shoals of weekend artists madly painting old bollards and bean poles in every conceivable position. Now, before you, too, go and drool over this rather untidy little place, a very real word of warning. As long ago as two hundred years, old Defoe summed it up characteristically:

'Swoul and Dunwich and Walberswick
All go in at one lousie creek.'

Forgive me, men of Southwold, this is just my fun but, well, there is just a grain of truth in it. 'Swoul' by the way, like the modern Sole for Sole Bay outside, has long been the local abbreviation for the full name which nobody could ever be bothered to pronounce. But the 'lousie Creek' served Dunwich long after its own harbour had been washed away and now saves Southwold from oblivion as a seaport. However, please ring up the harbourmaster before coming in or Mr. Pile, the Trinity House Pilot, if you want your vessel brought in because even the summer gales play impish tricks and I have seen a couple of mechanical diggers at work on a twenty yard wide pile of shingle at the harbour mouth that stood three feet above the surface at somewhere near high tide. The next gale may wash it away and dump it on Orfordness or on the bar but you never know. Normally, there is about three feet of water at LWS, so the best time is between half tide and high tide. Once the estuary is open, go in carefully hugging the north wall as there is a bad eddy, until the staging and speed limit board are astern. There are visitors' moorings upstream or you may pick up a buoy in mid-stream between the town slip and the bailey bridge until the Harbour Master tells you where best to go. There is a dinghy hard below the mooring stages on the south side but all your chandlery stores and the town are on the Southwold side to the north and remember, the ebb can run at seven knots when it really tries!

Southwold, as seen from Walberswick

The town is rather fun in spite of being constantly knocked about. It has spent most of its life dodging Dutch and French cannon balls and putting out fires – it has twice been burned down or partially at least. But there is something left for every taste. Have a drink at the *Harbour Inn* by the river to give you strength to climb the slope to the old town nestling round its lighthouse and take the children to see old 'Jack o' the clock' striking the hours on the Church with its pleasant painted rood screen and angels disporting themselves on the hammerbeam roof. There is a pleasant view from the hill over Reydon Marshes, the haunt of stooping kestrels and the patient heron. Seaward, I always think the view is invariably at its best after a good dinner and the water is settling down to that soft sort of purple velvet haze that is such a lasting memory of summer nights.

I never know which is the more beautiful, this or those brittle mornings at anchor, with no wind and perhaps a slight mist through which the rising sun searches out the favoured places and lights the window panes of ancient houses that stand on Gun Hill beyond the Green. A shimmer passes over the grey green saltings and ruffles the water along Black Shore and mixes up all the reflections of the masts and mooring posts in front of the old inn. Then the sun really gets a grip of the landscape and knocks sparks off the dewy sea lavender, turning the marshes beyond Buss creek into a riot of colour. To the west, Old Blythburgh Church stands up like some Rhineland castle. If you are up that way, the *White Hart Inn* is a fine old place and so, incidentally, are some of the houses in the village of Walberswick, not to mention its two reasonable inns. It is a great pity all the old Norfolk wherries have gone, they used to be a grand sight on the river.

If you like flowers, by the way, go for a walk along the cliffs in the direction of Dunwich and towards the end of June you will find that favourite of mine, the beautiful little burnet rose with its lovely petals and dainty leaflets trailing over the banks or blooming in great hummocks of colour. It used to like the ruins of the old monastry and so it should because the monks are said to have tended it well and named it the 'Holy Flower'. The Dunwich Rose, it is called locally and I have a shrewd notion that it much prefers this to *Pimpinellifolia,* which **is** what the clever boys call it.

Lowestoft

Now to Lowestoft – with somewhat mixed feelings. It has a long history, but you are quite safe as I am not allowed to inflict it on you here. Though in fairness to you and to Lowestoft, I must warn you not to expect the charm or colour of most of the places I have taken you into so far and I must admit we seldom go there. For the yachtsman it is a night's lodging on an even keel, rather than a goal for a party. It is in fact what it has grown up to be, an honest fishing port which still supplies most of the hinterland shops and I must admit to finding the coming and going and unloading of quayside fish markets great fun.

There are also still some charming, old spots like the quaint colony of pebble built cottages of the beach men and old red-roofed fish curing houses with net heating chambers in the vicinity of Ness Point, the most eastern point of England. This is a Lowestoft that had never heard of boarding houses, bathing beaches and Bingo Halls, and I would have a fair old guess that the fish curing rooms held barrels of much greater interest than herring or mackerel, every time a lugger crept in after dark with a suitable diversion being organised at the other end of the harbour. There is still a flavour of old Pegotty and David Copperfield about the place in spite of a number of really well kept public gardens and convenient inns.

Anyway, we haven't got there yet and, again the chart, because there are unpleasant banks. There is an inshore passage, one and a half to two cables wide, shown but, especially in poor visibility, I should go offshore and keep to the east of the Barnard Shoal off Benacre Ness. A useful tip is to keep Southwold lighthouse not less than 218° until Kessingland Church bears 297°. This, if they are visible, will keep you five cables off the shoal and if there is any sort of onshore wind you won't need the warning!

The Lowestoft entry is not difficult, except in strong onshore winds, if you follow the instructions. It is all very shallow, especially some nasty patches to the east of the South Road, so you can expect trouble in those winds during the ebb. Best then, if you have to enter, is to keep North Pier just shut in by the South Pier and shoot in on engine, meeting the eddy with the helm. You will see the yacht basin in the south west corner and the helpful club boatman is generally on hand to tell you where to anchor with stern warp to the promenade if inside, or tie bow to buoy and stern warp to hawser if in the outer tier. The *Royal Norfolk and Suffolk* is just ashore in front of you and the helpful steward will guide you to the visitors' book after which you need have no worries.

Great Yarmouth

You can, of course, also go to Yarmouth, Great Yarmouth, if you want. It is a worthy place, but not my idea of fun for yachtsmen. Tides run fast, anchoring is prohibited and the poor Harbourmaster may be hard put to find you a berth, but don't let me deter you from trying anything once. You can even escape into the Broads (as at Lowestoft) if you can squeeze in but I am afraid sailing days for a sea-going cruiser on the Broads are over.

Now this doesn't mean Great Yarmouth is a dull town; you have only to row as far as Haven Bridge and walk over to enjoy the sparkling expanse of Breydon Water on one side and in front you have not only the spire of the largest parish Church in England but the hospitable front of the *Old Star Hotel* on Hall Quay. You will agree it is a very fine old house, with its carved beams, Nelson Room and hall which was originally built by William Crowe when he was made town bailiff. Over the fireplace are the arms of the Spanish merchants. When Nelson landed on 6th November 1800, having just won the battle of the Nile, the local boys detached the horses and pulled his carriage through cheering streets to the old *Wrestlers Hotel* where there was one whale of a party to present the freedom of the borough. Beyond are the lovely old narrow 'rows' of the 'Norfolk grid-iron'. There is a flavour of Holland about much of Great Yarmouth; indeed it was this aspect which struck Dickens when he makes David Copperfield say to old Pegotty: 'that a mound might improve it', but when they got into the streets which 'smelt of fish and pitch and oakum and tallow and saw the sailors walking about', he felt, like us perhaps, that 'he had done the place an injustice'. The Dutch and East Anglian fishermen were for the most part on very friendly terms and there was even a 'Dutch Sunday' every third Sunday in September.

Now the Dutch are no longer welcome to 'wet their nets' on the coast or come to Yarmouth to load pickled herrings for the home market.

However, the quays along the river are still enjoyable in the evening, especially when the fishing boats are in, and the sun still sets like the Parsee's Hat 'with more than oriental splendour' across Breydon Water as you come back to your boat from *The Royal* or the *Two Bears* or the *Marine View*.

Tailpiece

Well, this is where we leave you and say goodbye and pleasant sailing – that is unless you feel like coming with us on our next cruising potter round the harbours and creeks of the Isle of Wight and the Hampshire coastline. Many of them are also favourite haunts of ours and perhaps we may persuade 'East coasters' to take a holiday round the corner. There is still plenty of room for all – 'if you know where to go' and that is just what we are going to talk to you about in our next book.

Meanwhile, I wonder which of the East coast creeks you will have enjoyed most by the end of next summer: the quiet evenings at Paglesham or Iken; the sea lavender and timeless spaciousness of Butley, or the pleasant coming and going of yachts and river craft on the Deben and a pint at the finish of a day's cruise at the *Ramsholt Arms* or the *Maybush*, or perhaps lunch time overlooking the barges and friendly anchorage from the *Butt and Oyster* bar parlour at Pin Mill. It is a pity we shall never know, but if we have helped you a little to make up your mind whether the East Coast would be fun for the annual cruise, and have saved you a bit of time by making suggestions as to where to go, it will have been worth a little trouble.

Bibliography

Pilot Books

The Cruising Association Handbook		Cruising Association, Revised Edition 1971
Coote, Jack H.	*East Coast Rivers*	Yachting Monthly, Latest Edition 1970
Wheeler, Cmdr. H.L.	*The Pilots Guide to the Thames Estuary*	Imray, Laurie, Norie, & Wilson, 1960

General Reading

Addison, William	*Essex Heyday*	Dent, 1949
Arnott, W.G.	*Suffolk Estuary*	Norman Adlard, 1950
Arnott, W.G.	*Alde Estuary*	Norman Adlard, 1952
Arnott, W.G.	*Orwell Estuary*	Norman Adlard, 1954
Baker, Granville	*Blyth Waters*	Heath Cranton, 1931
Benson, A.C.	*Edward Fitzgerald*	Macmillan, 1904
Clark, Roy	*Black Sailed Traders*	Putnam, 1961
Clarke, R. Rainbird	*East Anglia*	Thames & Hudson, 1960
Clodd, H.P.	*Aldeburgh*	Norman Adlard, 1959
Cooper, E.R.	*A Suffolk Coast Garland*	Heath Cranton, 1929
Dutt, W.A.	*Highways and Byways in East Anglia*	Macmillan, 1923
Dutt, W.A.	*Suffolk*	Methuen, 1904
Griffiths, Maurice	*The Magic of the Swatchways*	Conway Maritime, 1932
Roberts, A.W.	*Coaching Bargemaster*	Edward Arnold, 1949.

Index